BICYCLE
TOURING
MADE EASY

BICYCLE TOURING MADE EASY

Lise Krieger

VITESSE PRESS • MONTPELIER,VERMONT

Bicycle Touring Made Easy

Published by Vitesse Press
PMB 367, 45 State Street
Montpelier, Vermont 05601-2100

Library of Congress Cataloging-in-Publication Data

Krieger, Lise.
   Bicycle touring made easy / Lise Krieger
     p.cm
   Includes index.
   ISB N 0-941950-48-4
    1. Bicycle touring. I. Title

   GV1044 .K75 2002
   796.6'4--dc21

                     2001056876

Cover design by James Brisson

Manufactured in the United States of America

10 9 8 7 6 5 4 3 2 1

Distributed in the United States by Alan C. Hood, Inc. (717-267-0867)

For sales inquiries and special prices for bulk quantities, contact Vitesse Press at 802-229-4243 or write to the address above.

DEDICATION

For Laurel —
A true friend in this adventure called 'life.'

And for Mom and Dad who have always encouraged me to do
it all,
be it riding a bike or writing a book.

And for Corrina, who keeps getting back on.

CONTENTS

So, open this book, dream a little, load up your bike, and let's go for a ride!

My thanks go out to all of the people who have helped me with this project: Corrina Cuarenta, whose vision made this a publishable manuscript; my photo "models" Kyle Seaburg and Kara Morrow; John Courtnell, for his valuable editorial advice; Fred Wicke, for inspiring me to tour in the first place; Nancy Davidson, for...well...everything; my editor, Dick Mansfield, for giving me a chance and helping me with this process; and all of my riding buddies over the years — starting with my brothers, Michael and Peter, and including Amey, Christine, Sylvia, Scott, Laurel, Thilo, Karen A., Corrina, Tracie L., Sharon, Sidney, Christina, Kyle, Donna, Sandra, Dionne, Jenny, Rebekah, Lauren, Jessica, Tracy F., Kathy, Dawn, Karen W., Michael, and Arnie.

INTRODUCTION

I was in junior high school when the 'Great Gas Shortage' of the seventies hit the country. Not yet old enough to drive, I didn't have to worry about conserving precious fuel or waiting for hours in gas lines. I wasn't environmentally conscious back then and the school bus took me pretty much everywhere I needed to go. Nonetheless, the gas shortage worried me.

I was fortunate, at that age, to already have done some traveling. In an effort to expand our horizons, my parents would frequently pack my brothers and me in the Chevy station wagon for East Coast excursions. Those car treks instilled in me a love of travel and I couldn't imagine what life would be like if all of the gas tanks ran dry and I could never leave my back yard again.

Fortunately, my projections didn't materialize and I have since journeyed near and far in all types of fuel-powered vehicles. But if faced with a gas crunch today, I wouldn't panic as I did some twenty years earlier for I have since discovered the gratifying mobility of bicycle touring.

My first bike tour was the result of a deal made with my best friend, Laurel. It was 1980 and we were still in college, but we talked about touring the West Coast of the United States when we graduated. Though neither of us rode bikes regularly at the time and our fitness levels were embarrassing, we vowed to make the trip.

Nearly fifteen years passed before Laurel and I were finally astride our heavily laden bicycles, looking warily down a steep Seattle street. Our twelve hundred mile bike trip would take us from Victoria, B.C. to San Francisco via the coastlines of Washington, Oregon, and Northern California. We would sleep in a tent at state park campgrounds each night and cook our meals on a little gas stove. We would average sixty or so miles a day with only a couple of days off to rest. We would ride through the downpours of Washington rain forests, the scorching heat of California deserts and the relentless headwinds of coastal Oregon. We would feel pain in parts of our bodies that had never known it before and experience emotional highs and lows, energy slumps and charges. We would see sights that filled us with a reverence for nature. We would make friends and memories and ... we would make it.

Since that first tour I have traveled many miles on my bicycle and learned a great deal about bike touring. With that in mind, what follows is a book designed to give neophyte riders enough instruction and encouragement to propel them down the road of two-wheeled travel. So, open this book, dream a little, load up your bike, and let's go for a ride!

1 / Why Go Bike Touring

The magic of bicycle touring is that it gives you the opportunity to experience the world with all of your senses. It is about overcoming physical discomfort and feeling the rush of physical power. It is about seeing things that you would normally miss from inside a speeding car. It is about smelling the air and perceiving how it changes from mile to mile. It is about feeling the wind, the sun, the rain, the heat, and the cold on your skin. It is about enjoying food as fuel for your body. It is about focusing on the richness of the journey, not the destination. It is about living every moment of every day — mentally, physically, emotionally, and spiritually — not as a tourist, but as a participant.

Asians believe that every traveler is looking for some truth about himself or herself. You can't help but discover truths about yourself while on a bike tour. Like any challenging endeavor, riding a bicycle long distances will push you to grow in ways more than physical. You will become aware of your ability to tolerate discomfort and frustration. You will learn that you can push yourself farther than you ever thought possible. Your emotional strength will be challenged and enhanced. You will find how easy it is to feel satisfied, to be filled up.

You will also discover that the concept of time is greatly altered while on a bike tour. Unlike real life when an hour or a day can slip away without you being aware of it, on a bike you'll find yourself focused on the present, aware of the moments of a day as you experience them.

You will also notice that your experience of emotions will be heightened while on tour. The range and intensity of emotions that a person might experience in a week (or month for those stable types) will be felt in a day, or even an hour. While on tour, my daily moods often run the gamut from euphoria to sadness to anger to enthusiasm to silliness to quiet introspection. If examined from a clinical perspective, such mood swings might call for medication, but while on a bike tour, when one's sense of time is altered, this experience is normal. I find that while I spend a lot of time daydreaming during my hours in the saddle, I am also totally present, totally in touch with my body, my feelings, and my surroundings.

You will also become aware of the joy of simplicity. When I was a teenager I became interested in Eastern religions and philosophies. While this might seem an unusual interest for a teenage girl, it felt like a natural extension to my youthful search for happiness. I became very interested in Zen thought and though I probably did not have a clear concept of what it really was, I believed its truth lay in simplicity. I was able, at that point in my life, to enjoy things simply for what they were. As I grew older and my life became more complicated, nothing seemed simple. Though I still yearned for it, I had lost that ability to view the world in elementary terms by clouding my emotional vision with complexity.

Embarking on a bike tour lets me to return to an appreciation of the simple things in life. What a relief it is to only have a few possessions to worry about. What fun it is to feel the wind dry my sweat as I cruise down a hill. How lovely a hot shower feels at the end of a day. How good simple food tastes. Simple pleasures come for me: smelling the air with deep breaths, stopping to pet a sheep at the side of a field or watching an eagle soar across the sky, having freshly laundered clothes to wear, refueling my body with a good meal, sitting down on a rock to write in my journal, lying down to sleep in warmth of my sleeping bag. These pleasures will be yours, too.

Bike touring is not only a great way to travel and explore, it is also a definitive metaphor for life. There is pain and elation, hills to struggle up and hills to sail down. Sometimes you can only think of your destination and other times you can appreciate where you are. At times you feel discouraged and at other times, powerful and self-assured. Sometimes it is fun, at other times, it's the pits. Like life, a bike tour will give you many gifts, some of which will be appreciated during the moment, and others that will be appreciated only later in retrospect.

Happy riding.

2 / Planning Your Tour

A bike tour can take many forms. It can be a foreign or domestic tour, one that includes camping out or the comforts of a hotel, one that immerses you in the wilderness or in a tourist mecca. The tour can be an easy, low-mileage, no-hill experience, or one that includes the challenges of harsh weather and mountainous terrain. It can be a tour designed and run by a touring company, or one that you plan and execute on your own. With all of these options, one must consider a number of questions before starting the initial planning stages.

Bicycle touring opens up a world of travel options

Helpful Hints
Questions to Ask Yourself When Planning a Tour

1. Where do you want to go?
    Do you wish to visit historical sites?
    Do you prefer cities to countryside?
    Do you want to immerse yourself
    in a culture different than your own?
    Do you like tourist attractions?
    Do you prefer wilderness?
    Do you wish to be in highly populated
    areas or in isolation?
    Do you like a combination of options?

2. How hard do you want to work?
    Do you want to carry your own gear?
    Do you wish to set up camp every night?
    Do you prefer the comfort of hotels and inns?
    Do you like the challenge of hills?
    Do you prefer a flat, temperate ride?
    Do you want to ride on paved roads or unpaved?

3. What are your time limits and budget?
    Do you have an extended vacation?
    Do you wish to spend a lot of money or a little?
    Do you want to start from your own backyard
    or travel to your starting point?
    Do you want to travel in a circle
    or start and stop in different locations?

4. With whom do you wish to travel?
    Do you have a potential riding partner?
    Do you prefer to travel with large groups
    or in smaller ones?
    Do you want to ride alone?

5. What will you eat? (See Chapter 9)

Bike Tour Operators

The first question you should ask yourself is whether you want to plan and execute your trip independently or use tour operators who have trips designed for varying degrees of difficulty and service. The most extensive (and expensive) will plan your route, haul your gear, arrange your lodging and meals, and even pick you up in a van (called SAG wagons — Support and Gear) when you are too tired to carry on. The more adventurous biker might opt for a camping tour in which the operators set up camp and feed you. Some tours are theme or education oriented, some address specific age groups and genders. Trip lengths range from a weekend to months long and offer itineraries worldwide. This is a great option for many cyclists.

Helpful Hints
Some Pros and Cons of Guided Bike Tours

Pros	**Cons**
–Traveling with a large group	–Traveling with a large group
–The planning is done for you	–Lack of flexibility & spontaneity
–Your gear is carried for you	–It costs more

Whatever your preference, there is a tour designed for you. Outdoor sports and adventure magazines are a great resource for investigating biking trips. Adventure Cycling Association publishes a manual called *The Cyclists' Yellow Pages*, which lists national and international tour operators, in addition to other valuable information. The League of American Bicyclists offers the *Tourfinder Catalogue*. There are a multitude of cycling related websites and newsgroups that offer valuable information about tours, including local rides, cross-country trips and tours with commercial touring companies. As bicycle touring has grown in popularity, so has the bike tour operator industry. You won't have to look far for a trip that will suit your needs.

Adventure Cycling Association
150 E. Pine Street
P.O. Box 8308
Missoula, MT 59807
(406) 721-8754
(800) 721-8719
info@adventurecycling.org
www.adv-cycling.org

League of American Bicyclists
1612 K Street NW, Suite 401
Washington, D.C. 20006
(202) 822-1333
bikeleague@bikeleague.org
www.bikeleague.org

Charity Rides

Another wonderful way to participate in a fully supported tour is through the various charity rides that are available. While local fundraising rides have been offered for years, the concept of long-distance charity rides have become increasingly popular in recent years, starting with the Tanqueray American AIDS Ride series. These rides, organized by Dan Pallota Teamworks are offered throughout the country and range from three-day, 300 mile events to seven-day 800 mile events.

The 3000 or so participants get a fully supported tour through some of the most scenic areas of America, with rest and food stops every 15 miles. SAG wagons carry their gear, and there's more food than any of them can eat along with comfortable camps at night complete with tents, catered meals, entertainment, hot showers, massage therapists, bike mechanics, and much more. In exchange for these amenities, the riders raise a significant amount of money and push themselves to ride their bikes an impressive number of miles.

AIDS Ride Information http://www.aidsride.org

Charity rides feature great organization and rider support

For anyone who is interested in trying a long-distance ride and would like to help raise money for a good cause, these and other charity rides like them are a great opportunity.

Planning Your Own Trip

If you are a do-it-yourselfer, or have a tighter budget to manage, you can design your own trip. The first step is deciding where you want to go. Of course, the most economical way to tour would be to leave from your own home. If you think you've seen all your area has to offer, remember that when traveling by bike, you will see things that you have previously overlooked and travel down roads you may have never explored, turning a local journey into a new, eye-opening adventure. If, however, you need a change of scenery, you can transport your bike and gear to your destination via car, train or plane.

Whatever your route, you need to consider the climate for the time of year you plan to ride, the terrain and the overall distance you intend to cover. Research weather trends, look at topographical and road maps, and talk to other people who have toured in that region.

Bike Touring Guidebooks

The bike touring guidebooks that are on the market are a valuable resource. These cover specific tour routes and spell out every necessary route detail, almost down to the bumps in the road. Many of them do not, however, give information about tourist sites, lodging and restaurants, so it is a good idea to use other travel guides for additional research. Because of the weight and bulk of these books, it is best to photocopy or write down the information on a small notepad. One person I met on tour had torn the necessary pages out of his books. At the end of his trip he would slip them back into the books and save them for the next time.

I did not carry such a guidebook on the West Coast ride, but I have since purchased one to research an East Coast trip. While I will probably continue to carry road maps for the sake of simplicity, these guidebooks are a worthwhile investment as well.

Adventure Cycling Association Maps

The Adventure Cycling Association (*see page 26*) is a great place to exchange ideas with other cyclists, find riding partners, buy used equipment, and share stories. When planning for my first long trip, the first thing I did was to buy bike route maps from ACA. While the information I received by joining was helpful, and I would recommend a membership highly, I found the maps too detailed to decipher with ease. When describing routes through more populated towns and cities, the Adventure Cycling maps listed every turn by street name, so I found myself continually stopping to look at the map. While a more experienced rider may be able to ride and read a map at the same time, it was enough that I was able to keep my heavily loaded bike upright. Don't get me wrong — these maps are detailed and accurate to a fault, and will surely appeal to many individuals. But I decided to give the Adventure Cycling Association maps to another rider, bought state road maps instead, and when approaching a city, aimed myself in the general direction of my destination. Though this technique added a few more miles to my trip, it was easier than stopping to read a map every three minutes.

State Road and Bicycle Maps

Some states have specific bike route maps that are distributed for free at Chambers of Commerce. Call or write ahead and they will gladly send you maps, camping guides, and other tourist information.

Many states publish specific maps for bikers. Oregon's map, for instance, lays out the coastal route in large print, indicating mileage, and the location of campgrounds, State Parks, Youth Hostels, and bike shops. It also blueprints the width of the shoulder of the road — invaluable information when riding side by side with behemoth logging trucks and motor homes.

An elevation chart is another feature unique to the Oregon map: it

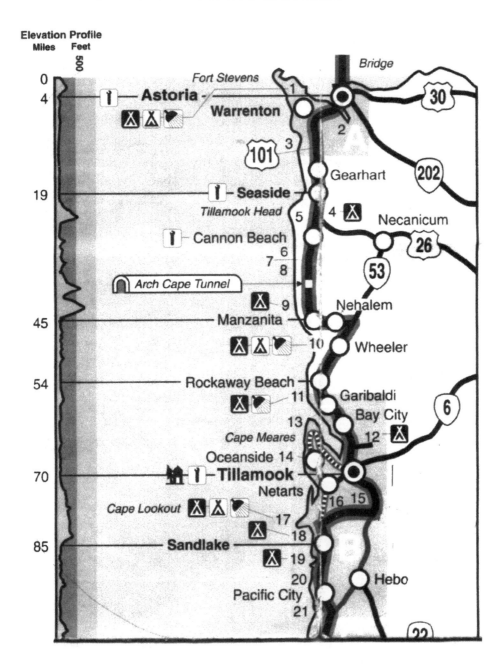

State Bicycle Map - Oregon

enabled us to see what mountain climbs lay ahead of us each day. Some people would prefer to not be aware of that information and just be surprised each time they reached the base of a significant hill. But I found it helpful in planning my daily mileage — a day of mountain riding will probably be a day during which you log fewer miles than usual.

State road maps also indicate the location of state campgrounds, while specific biking maps usually list commercial campsites and Youth Hostels as well. If you intend to camp out during your ride, it is critical that you locate on your map two or more possible stopping sites for the night, within a reasonable riding distance. During busier travel seasons campgrounds tend to fill up quickly, and some state parks and most commercial sites, when full, do turn bikers away. More than once, I have arrived at a campground, exhausted, hungry and ready to quit for the day, only to find a "no vacancy" sign hanging on the gates. Another look at the map informed me that we should have stopped at the KOA ten miles earlier, for the next area was another fifteen. At the end of a long day that is a most unpleasant prospect. With cell phone usage and coverage more prevalent, many prudent tourers will call ahead during the day.

Planning Your Daily Distance

When planning your daily distance, it is important to consider the purpose of your trip and the length of time you have allotted for travel. Are you riding to accomplish a goal or to take in the sites? Do you want to reach a specific destination in a certain period of time, or are your plans more flexible?

I calculated the distance for my first long tour incorrectly. I estimated the distance of our proposed route from Canada to Mexico to be about eleven hundred miles, border to border, but realized halfway through Oregon that it was more like seventeen hundred. I think when adding up the distance for each state, I forgot Oregon. Oops.

Laurel and I struggled for a number of days with the issue of whether to push ourselves to achieve our original goal or to ride at a reasonable pace and enjoy the trip. Ultimately, however, it was the advice of Thilo, a German rider traveling from Alaska to Arizona, who said, "if you push it to the Mexican border, you will have the satisfaction of that, but you will lose the beauty of the experience as you go along. Bike touring is about the journey, not the destination. You have to stop and smell the roses."

So we rode to San Francisco instead — an admirable 2000 kilometers — averaging about 100 kilometers a day. Some people put more daily miles behind them, and some fewer, but we found it to be a comfortable pace for us. We met a few people who were riding one hundred or so miles a day, which is impressive, but they had no time to take in the sights, socialize at night in the campgrounds, or just relax. Remember that you will be riding day-in, day-out, on bicycles loaded with up to seventy pounds of gear. It is easy to burn out. I have tried a couple of eighty-mile days during my fully loaded tours but found that they wiped me out too much to maintain consistent mileage in the days following. And the rare twenty to thirty mile day is too short. It is a matter of finding what works for you.

Find an average distance per day that works for you

Determining Your Average Speed

In order to plan your route mileage, it is important to know your average speed. A comfortable rate for most riders on fully loaded bikes is ten to twelve miles per hour. While ten miles up the road in a car would take a matter of minutes, on a bike it takes an hour. Take a few minutes periodically to check your progress during the day and adjust plans accordingly.

Check your progress during the day and adjust plans accordingly

With maps that don't spell out mileage data in detail, I have improvised a system that works fairly well. Using my finger between the first and second knuckle as a ruler allows me to measure out fifty mile distances (give or take ten) on the map and thus determine how many days it will take to get from one point to the next. The Oregon coast, for instance, is 363 miles long, and at fifty miles or more a day, I could make it through in a week. Depending on your daily mileage and time schedule, you can adjust your plans accordingly. And don't forget to schedule in some rest days!

Helpful Hints

Do-It-Yourself Trip Planning Summary

1. Determine how many days your trip will be.
2. Decide where you want to go.
3. Estimating 40-50 miles a day, depending on terrain, determine the overall mileage you will cover during your tour.
(Don't forget to include rest days.)
4. Determine your starting and stopping points.
5. Obtain maps, guidebooks, camping information, and advice from other riders to determine your route.
6. Make travel arrangements to transport you and your bike to and from your destination.

Logging Your Route

As a writer and compulsive recorder of memories, it is important to me to log the routes I have traveled. For this purpose I bring two different colored highlighter pens and each day trace my route with an alternating color. There is really no reason to do this except to see where I have been. Those maps are now in my photo album along with other mementos of my trips. Bring some highlighters along. They weigh next to nothing and take up very little space.

Transporting Your Bike

If you are planning a tour that begins from a distant destination, it is relatively easy to transport your bike. Airlines will always check your bike, usually for a fee of around $50 each way. The bicycle must be packed before you arrive at the airport, and if you've ever watched baggage handlers, you know that it must be packed well.

There are a number of travel cases on the market for bikes. Made of either hard or soft exteriors and foam-padded interiors, and ranging from $100.00 to $400.00, these cases offer your bike the best protection. But, if your starting and ending points are different locations, you will have to leave your carrying case behind — an expensive and undesirable option. Instead, go to your local bike shop and they will gladly give you an empty bicycle box for free.

Where To Find It
Travel Cases For Bicycles

Bike Nashbar
4111 Simon Road
Youngstown, OH 44512
(800) NASHBAR
http://www.nashbar.com

Delta Cases
http://stores.yahoo.com/deltacases

Performance Bike
P.O. Box 2741
Chapel Hill, NC 27514
(800) 727-2453
http://www.performancebike.com

Pricepoint
(800) 774-2376
http://www.pricepoint.com

Packing Your Bike for Transportation

While your local bike shop will pack your bicycle in a cardboard box for a minimal fee, it is better if you learn to do it yourself. Once you arrive at your destination you will have to rebuild your bike and then disassemble it for the trip home, so if you don't become familiar with the process you will find yourself in a predicament. Airports have a variety of stores, but a bike shop usually isn't one of them. It is a simple process and the more you practice dismantling your bike, the more comfortable you will be when it is time to make repairs.

To pack your bike, follow these steps:

1. Apply tape to the handlebar stem and seatpost before removing to mark the correct position. This will save you time when reassembling.

2. Remove the wheels and let some of the air out of the tires to prevent explosion from changing air pressure.

3. Remove seatpost.

4. Remove pedals (remember the left pedal screws off clockwise.)

5. Remove handlebars and stem. Cover stem with foam pipe insulation or padding of some sort.

6. Support wheel dropouts by placing an old hub or piece of fitted wood where the wheel attached to avoid bending.
7. Wrap frame with rags or newspaper to prevent scratching (clothing works well, too.)
8. Tie or tape handlebars to top tube of frame.
9. With a soft case or box, remove rear derailleur, wrap in padding (rags will do) and strap to frame.

10. Put bike in box and use more padding, straps, and tape to secure it various parts.
11. Tape box securely and write your name, address and phone number on it.

When you claim your bike on arrival, open it up to check for any visible damage. After reassembling it, take a short test-ride to work out any kinks. Make sure all bolts are tight and brakes are adjusted before you ride any distance.

You can also pack some of your gear in your bike box. Clothing and sleeping bags, wrapped in plastic, make for good padding.

3 / Training for Your Ride

You do not have to be a super-athletic mega jock to take a bike tour, but you do need to train. However, if you are tempted to pick up a training manual at your local bookstore, keep in mind that these are usually written for competitive bikers whose level of fitness far exceeds that of more leisurely riders. The training programs outlined can be overwhelming to the ordinary bike enthusiast. While your own training program can be less intense, it still should be demanding and challenging. The point is to be able to go touring with as little discomfort as possible so your energy can be spent enjoying instead of suffering.

Riding

Obviously, the best way to prepare for a tour is to ride. Ride daily. Ride to work, ride to the grocery store, ride many miles, ride a few. Just ride. Make your bike a part of you. Soon it will seem easier to ride your bike somewhere than to put your car in gear.

Whether you are planning a 1500-mile tour or a 50-mile tour, you need to be able to ride the distance of your average daily mileage a number of days in a row. You should start your training plan by calculating the amount of time you have to train before your trip and working up to your planned daily mileage. Remember that you will be touring on a heavier bike, so if you plan to average around 50 miles a day, it is a good idea to boost your training average up ten or more miles, so ride some 100 kilometer training rides.

Increase your mileage gradually during the initial phases of training. It is best to ride four times a week, but if your work schedule interferes, you can make the weekday rides short ones, and the weekend rides longer. If your workplace has a shower and it is possible to commute, try to do so a few times a week. When the weather allows, I get on my bike at 5:30 a.m. for the ten-mile ride to work a few times a week. I bring my clothes and toiletries the day before, shower in the girls' locker room (I'm a teacher) and run on exercise energy for the rest of the day. It's a great way to start the day, it benefits the environment, and is perfect way to incorporate training into my daily routine. If commuting is not possible but you can squeeze a five or ten mile ride in during the week, do so. Even short rides are beneficial. Also, getting used to being in the saddle on consecutive days is an important element of training for a tour.

Load up your panniers for some training rides

Weekend rides should be longer. Start with ten to twenty-mile rides and gradually increase your mileage to fifty. What might seem overwhelming in the beginning will become easier. A ten-mile ride is really nothing to someone who is fit, and can be completed in less than an hour, so the eventual fifty-miler will become a morning jaunt instead of a chore.

If you need the motivation of a rider partner, ask your local bike shop or check on-line for area bike clubs. These are usually a group of non-competitive riders who want to share their love of biking with each other. They generally have regularly scheduled weekend rides, which vary in length and difficulty. It's a great way to meet people, too.

During your training, do not avoid hills! Even if you hate hills, as many of us do, you are going to encounter them during a tour. Hill riding will make you stronger and increase your stamina and confidence. You don't have to race up hills, or stand in the pedals and jam — simply ride along steadily until you reach the top. Remember: slow and steady wins the race.

As you progress, start putting some loads on your bike. You'll note in the training schedule which follows, I suggest doing this during the last month of your preparation. You can start earlier than that with light loads, and get used to handling a loaded bike.

Training rides are good chances to get comfortable with drinking from water bottles while riding, changing hand positions to avoid numbness, getting familiar with gear changes, and riding with a training partner. Use the time to read maps and work with your bike computer. Train the brain and the body.

Make sure to factor rest days into your training schedule. Over-training is counterproductive since your muscles need time to heal in between workouts. Too much training will only lead to exhaustion and/or injury. If you are riding on a daily basis, alter longer distance rides with shorter ones, and take a day off after an especially challenging ride.

Helpful Hints
Sample Training Plan
(Three months until take-off)

Month 1

Sun.	Mon.	Tues.	Wed.	Thurs.	Fri.	Sat.
1 10 mi.	2	3 5-10 mi.	4	5 5-10 mi.	6	7 15 mi.
8 15 mi.	9	10 5-10 mi.	11	12 5-10 mi.	13	14 20 mi.
15 20 mi.	16	16 5-10 mi.	18	19 5-10 mi.	20	21 25 mi.
22 25 mi.	23	24 5-10 mi.	25	26 5-10 mi.	27	28 30 mi.
29 30 mi.	30					

Month 2

Sun.	Mon.	Tues.	Wed.	Thurs.	Fri.	Sat.
		1 5-10 mi.	2	3 5-10 mi.	4	5 35 mi.
6 35 mi.	7	8 5-10 mi.	9	10 5-10 mi.	11	12 40 mi.
13 40 mi.	14	15 5-10 mi.	16	17 5-10 mi.	18	19 45 mi.
20 45 mi.	21	22 5-10 mi.	23	24 5-10 mi.	25	26 50 mi.
27 50 mi.	28	29 5-10 mi.	30			

Month 3

Sun.	Mon.	Tues.	Wed.	Thurs.	Fri.	Sat.
				1 5-10 mi.	2	3 55 mi.
4 55 mi.	5	6 5-10 mi.	7	8 5-10 mi.	9	10 25 mi. L
11 30 mi. L	12	13 5-10 mi. L	14	15 5-10 mi. L	16	17 40 mi. L
18 30 mi. L	19	20 5-10 mi. L	21	22 5-10 mi. L	23	24 20 mi.
25 10 mi.	26	27 5 mi.	28 Rest	29 Rest	30 Take Off!	

* L markes the rides where you should load your panniers

** Empty days can be used for strength training or cross-training, but DON'T FORGET TO REST!

If work or family constraints make it difficult for you to keep to this schedule, or you miss a few days here and there, don't give up—you will still be able to tour comfortably. Just having ridden somewhat consistently will prepare you sufficiently, and though you may have a slower start, you will get more fit as the tour progresses.

Cross Training

Cross training is always beneficial. Not only does it relieve the boredom associated with doing the same activity everyday, it can also give the bicycling muscles and joints a rest. Walking, swimming, running, jumping rope, playing tennis or any other exercise will enhance your performance. Just do not rely on these non-bicycling activities for your sole form of training — you must ride your bike!

Strength Training

Stronger leg muscles make for easier riding. By increasing your muscle mass, you will experience greater endurance and, therefore, less fatigue. While using free weights or weight machines is ideal, if you don't have access to such equipment, you can do exercises at home. Deep knee bends, lunges, and calf raises are some of the leg workouts that will help.

Deep Knee Bends

Lunges

Calf Raises

If you learn to use weights and weight machines, squats, leg presses, leg extensions and curls are good for upper leg strengthening.

Squats

Don't forget to work your stomach, arm and back muscles. Though they might not make the wheels go around, these often neglected areas are important muscle groups used in riding. These exercises can be done with or without weights.

Leg Press

Leg Extension

Indoor Training

If you are planning a spring trip and winter weather prohibits outdoor training, there are dozens of wind or resistance trainers on the market for indoor training. These trainers keep your bike stationary while you pedal by elevating or eliminating the rear wheel. You may want to use the bike you'll be touring on so that you can get used to the seat and handlebar setup. Others like to use a less expensive bike on a wind trainer to avoid wear and tear on their "baby." You can use your gears to increase or decrease tension, simulating hills and straightaways. There are videos you can watch while you ride and let you "tour" without leaving the house. For most, a television or a pair of headphones helps you get through the boredom of inside riding. The kilometers you log in your basement will pay off come spring when it's time to hit the road. There are a number of trainers on the market to choose from, and while they tend to be expensive, they are a worthwhile investment for people who live in colder winter climes.

Rollers are another option, but are a bit trickier to master. A roller requires that you balance your bike on moveable tubes, forcing you to pedal and stay upright at the same time. A roller is often the choice of racers who wish to enhance their technique as well.

Where To Find It:
Wind Trainers & Rollers

Bike Nashbar
4111 Simon Road
Youngstown, OH 44512
(800) NASHBAR
http://www.nashbar.com

Performance Bike
P.O. Box 2741
Chapel Hill, NC 27514
(800) 727-2453
http://www.performancebike.com

Pricepoint
(800) 774-2376
http://www.pricepoint.com

BikepartsUSA
http://www.bikepartsUSA.com

Riding on an indoor trainer is effective but can also be exceptionally boring. Many people go to fitness centers to take *Spinning* classes which are entertaining and extremely challenging. Astride specially constructed stationary bicycles, *'Spinners'* ride with a group of people in a darkened room, surrounded by loud, heart-pumping music.

Classes are an hour to an hour and a half long, and are guaranteed to give you a total body, bicycling-specific workout. Plus, there is an instructor to motivate you, which helps when you feel like heading to the shower too soon.

4 / Keeping Comfortable

Being fit is only half the battle. Long distance biking can cause discomforts that are more debilitating than fatigue and muscle pain. Fortunately there are ways to minimize the pain.

Your Seat

Seat and crotch pain is perhaps the most uncomfortable situation with which riders deal. Whether you are a man or a woman, your crotch and seat will take a beating when riding for a long time and no matter the condition of your muscles, if you can't sit you can't ride. It is essential to take proper care of this sensitive area.

Some discomforts such as bruising and the occasional saddle-sore can be expected, but numbness and impotence should not be tolerated. Numbness in both men and women is caused by compression of blood vessels and, unlike a foot that falls asleep and returns to normal after a few minutes, many bikers have reported that numbness has persisted for day, weeks, or even months after a long ride.

Buying the Proper Bike Seat

First of all, make sure you have the right seat. The seat that comes with your bike is most likely not the best one for you. People's anatomies differ according to their gender and individual body structure, as do their riding styles and tolerance levels, and seats should purchased with these factors in mind. Common to the anatomies of both men and women are the ischial tuberosities, or the 'sit bones.' Padded with muscle and fat, these bones allow you to sit on wide, flat surfaces without damaging the sensitive, nerve-filled organs between them. A bicycle seat, however, is neither wide nor flat, so it presses on the sensitive nerves and arteries that are supposed to be protected by the sit bones.

Men who spend a lot of time on a bicycle seat have reported numbness, and in more extreme cases, loss of erection and impotence. This is a result of the pressure of the bicycle seat compressing the arteries that travel to the penis. Usually, the bruised arteries expand again, but sometimes they don't. (Got your attention yet?)

A touring seat for men — note the recessed center section

Women also feel numbness when riding for long periods of time, and though this numbness might not cause the same long-term health effects, it is painful. Women, however, are more likely to experience saddle sores than men due to moisture and tissue sensitivity. Not only is this quite uncomfortable, it also carries the risk of infection.

Years ago there were few options in bike seats and none specifically made for the separate needs of men and women. Now, however, seats have been designed to promote not only comfort, but also health, and the market is full of seats of varying sizes, shapes and styles.

The factors to consider when purchasing a bike seat are the width, cushioning, material with which the seat is made, your gender, and individual body shape.

Width

The width of a saddle should be considered in proportion to the space between the rider's sit bones. If the seat is too narrow, the sit bones will drape over the edge, forcing the sensitive tissues in the middle to bear all of the rider's weight. If the seat is too wide, chafing of the inner thigh is likely, especially when riding in hot weather.

Women should consider a wider seat than men, since their sit bones are positioned farther apart. But width is not the only consideration, so read on before you run out to buy a new seat!

Padding

A bicycle seat with more padding, it would seem, should be more comfortable than one without. But cushioning is not necessarily the best indicator for comfort. In fact, a thick foam or gel may actually bulge in the center as it's pressed down on the sides, increasing pressure precisely where you don't want it. Excessive gel padding may also contribute to chafing due to its tendency to shift and slide. Generally, the padding of a good pair of bicycle shorts is sufficient.

Seat Material

Two main materials are used to construct bicycle seats: padded plastic or leather. A plastic seat is made by attaching a hard plastic base to a metal frame, and padding it with a gel or other soft material. Depending on the style and make of the saddle, the cover will be vinyl, vinyl-covered cloth or Lycra. Proponents of plastic saddles claim they are lighter, easier to care for, and easier to find on the market. Most of them have also never ridden on a leather saddle because they consider them antiquated and uncomfortable due to lack of padding.

Leather seats are made by stretching a thick piece of leather to three points on a frame — two on the curved back bridge and one on the nose of the saddle.

Leather saddles stretch, flex and mold themselves to your particular anatomy, just like a good pair of shoes or gloves. Proponents of the leather saddle claim that it is the absence of the rigid plastic base and its ability to transform itself that makes it the most comfortable saddle on the market.

New Seat Designs

There are a few new seat designs on the market to address the concerns and discomforts of riders. The first is the cut-away seat, which has a hole cut into the nose of the saddle where the rider's sensitive areas rest.

Cut-away Saddle

The reasoning behind this saddle is that less direct pressure on this sensitive area will cause less discomfort and long-term damage. These seats are designed differently for men and women.

A saddle designed for women

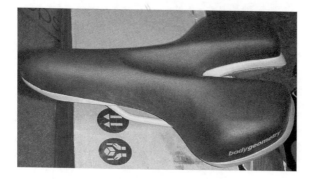

A saddle designed for men

Cost

Bicycle seats can run anywhere between twenty dollars and one hundred and fifty. While you don't have to spend a fortune on a bicycle seat, you should keep in mind the importance of comfort. Some bicycle shops allow customers to borrow seats for test rides, or if that option is not available, you can always try a seat that belongs to a friend. You're going to spend a lot of time on it, so make sure that you get a seat that will feel good at the start, and the end, of the day.

Where To Find It
Bicycle Seats

Aardvark Cycles
(877) 346-6098
www.aardvarkcycles.com/saddles.html

Bike Nashbar
4111 Simon Road
Youngstown, OH 44512
(800) NASHBAR
http://www.nashbar.com

Performance Bike
P.O. Box 2741
Chapel Hill, NC 27514
(800) 727-2453
http://www.performancebike.com

Pricepoint
(800) 774-2376
http://www.pricepoint.com

Spongy Wonder Inc.
2 Woodside Drive
Riverview, New Brunswick,
E1B 4G9 Canada
(877) 977-7328
http://www.spongywonder.com

Terry Precision Cycling
1704 Wayneport Road
Macedon, NY 14502
(800) 289-8379
http://www.terrybicycles.com

Seat Adjustment

Proper seat adjustment is also critical. Height, seat angle and the distance from the handlebars need to be set for each individual. While a good bike shop can help you with these adjustments, it is important to know how to do it yourself.

Height

Seat height is best set so that the leg is nearly fully extended, but not locked, with the heel slightly below the ball of the foot when the pedal is at the bottom of the stroke. A seat that is too high will cause the rider's hips to rock back and forth as his or her legs stretch to reach the pedals. Such rocking will contribute to putting pressure on the sensitive areas of your crotch as well as exacerbate any chafing that is likely to occur. Have a friend ride behind you to determine if your hips are remaining still while you pedal.

Correct leg position while seated

Adjusting Seat Height

Front/Back Positioning

Bicycle seats can also be slid nearer to or farther from the handlebars. The seat should be positioned so that a plumb line dropped from the knob beneath the kneecap intersects the forward pedal axle when the pedals are held horizontal.

It is important not to use front/back seat positioning to compensate for a bike frame that is too long for your torso. This adjustment should be made by installing a different sized stem or buying a bike with a shorter top tube length.

Women tend to have shorter torsos than men do and when they buy an improperly fitted bike; they may have to lean farther forward to reach the handlebars. This can put more direct pressure on the labia or too much weight on the arms. Front-back positioning will not correct this problem completely if the frame is too long.

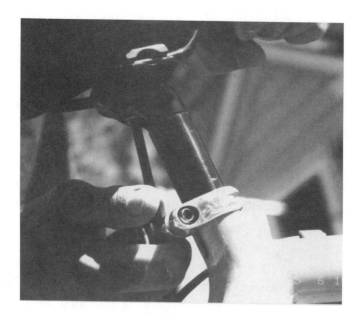

Adjusting front/back seat position

Seat Angle

The seat should be positioned horizontally, allowing for *slight* variations depending on preference. Often, men prefer to tilt the saddle slightly back, while women go for a forward tilt. Tipping the front of the saddle up too far, however, will put more pressure on the soft tissues as the body leans forward into the seat. The sit bones are also prone to greater discomfort in this position as more pressure is being forced upon them. Tilting a seat too far down in front, on the other hand, may cause the rider to slide too far forward, also putting pressure on the sensitive areas. It is best if the rider's weight is distributed evenly on the saddle, with or without cut-away designs. Seat angle and front/back positioning can be adjusted using the same bolt (see above photo)

Bike Shorts

Another common problem is abrasion. Raw spots and infections are caused by clothing abrading the skin as you slide around in your seat, and bacteria trapped in the warm, moist environment. The best way to avoid both is to wear padded bike shorts. They fit snugly so no excess material can bunch up and rub, and are anatomically cut so they will be more comfortable in the bent over riding position. They provide cushioning and are made with the seams positioned away from sensitive areas. Bike shorts also draw sweat away from the skin, keeping you as dry as possible.

It is also important to keep your crotch as clean and dry as possible. This is especially important for women to avoid yeast infections. Padded bike shorts are meant to be worn *without* underwear as underwear causes chafing and traps bacteria. Riding shorts should be washed after each use and dried inside out. While on tour, bring enough shorts so that you can wear a clean pair each day.

You should also remove your biking shorts as soon as possible at the end of the day and shower or wash yourself. Some people carry Baby-Wipes or other convenient hygiene products for use when a shower is not immediately available. Other products that bikers use to ease chafing are Vaseline or A & D Ointment. Many people smear these lubricants on liberally before each ride to provide an extra barrier against chafing whether or not they have a rash. Especially beneficial to women are Vagisil, Gyne-Lotrimin and other feminine products that will help offset the inevitable bacterial build-up.

Knees

Knee pain can be alleviated by proper bike fit, seat height and specific riding techniques. While crotch pain can be unpleasant, it will not necessarily force you to stop a ride. Knees, however, are critical. It is easy to injure a knee while clocking mile after mile on a bike. And once your knee goes, your tour is finished.

Chondromalacia

The knee joint is formed by the interconnection of four bones: the thigh bone, the knee cap and the two lower legs bones, the tibia and fibula, which are positioned on either side. These bones are covered on the ends with cartilage, where the joint motion occurs. A thick shock-absorbing cartilage pad, the meniscus, is positioned between the femur and tibia. The joint is lubricated by fluid and held together by tough connective tissues.

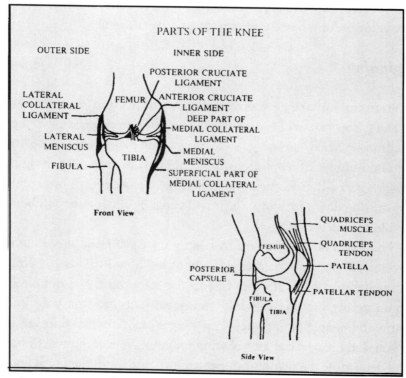

A common cycling-related knee injury is called chondromalacia, which is due to wearing down the protective cartilage covering the bones. This feels like a sandpaper-like grinding when you place the palm of your hand on your kneecap and bend the knee back and forth. Other knee complaints are ligament and tendon damage.

Seat Height

As mentioned in the section on seat comfort, the height of your saddle should be set so that the leg is nearly fully extended without being locked. The heel should hang slightly below the ball of the foot when the pedal is at the bottom of the stroke. (See photo on page 57).

When adjusting your seat height, avoid changing it drastically or you risk injury. The tendons and ligaments that support your knee-caps are accustomed to the seat height at which you've been riding. Therefore, be sure to adjust the height in tiny increments and ride at those levels for a few days before changing it again.

Spinning

A common mistake newcomers make is not to "spin" enough when cycling. You can avoid knee strain and chondromalacia by using a technique called 'spinning,' – keeping your pedal cadence up to a certain number of revolutions per minute. Rather than pushing the biggest gear as hard as you can (called "gear mashing" in bikespeak), try shifting down to a lower gear and pedaling at a higher number of revolutions per minute.

The general rule is to try to keep your cadence at about eighty revolutions per minute. (Periodically to see how I'm doing, I count my pedal strokes for my right pedal for 30 seconds and double it.) Spinning uses significantly less energy, eases up stress on your knee joints and enables you to pedal far longer before exhaustion sets in. If you don't have a cadence reading on your cycle computer to help you determine the revolutions per minute, just count the pedal revolutions every so often. Another good check is this: if you seem to be pumping too hard and spinning too slowly, shift down...or get off and push.

Cleat Adjustment

For riders who use clipless pedals, it is important to position the shoe cleats to compensate for the natural angle of your feet. Some people are duck-footed and some are pigeon-toed and if the cleats are adjusted in a way that opposes the anatomical structure, the rider's knees will be affected. Many clipless pedals come with what is called "float", which allows the rider's foot to rotate slightly. This type of pedal can help alleviate knee pain.

Clipless pedals without float (l) and with float (r)

Strengthening Your Knees

Stronger thigh and hamstring muscles will help to take some of the strain off of your knees. Specific exercises are included in the previous chapter on training.

Achilles Tendons

The Achilles tendon is at the back of the ankle, connecting the calf muscle to the heel. If you are experiencing pain in these tendons, it is usually the result of *ankling* which is the process of flexing your ankles as you pedal instead of keeping your foot still. This is often the result of having the seat too high, which forces the rider to point his/her toes during the downstroke.

Ankling can cause Achilles tendon pain

Having your cleats positioned too far forward on your shoes or pedaling with your toes can also cause Achilles tendinitis.

Stretching exercises are another way to help prevent Achilles tendon problems. Stand up, keep the pedals even, and gently lower your heel, feeling the easy stretch in the back of your lower leg. You can do them before the ride, during the ride, and after the ride.

On-the-bike tendon stretch

Necks

Neck pain is most often the result of poor posture, whether forced by poor bike fit or helmet and eyeglass positioning.

Helmet and Eyeglass Position

A sharp backward angle of the neck will invariably cause severe neck problems, so it is critical to make adjustments to avoid this. Occasionally a rider will wear his/her helmet tilted too far down on the forehead, forcing the rider to bend his/her neck to look up. It is important to fit the helmet properly to suit riding style. Glasses that rest too far forward on the nose can also cause this problem.

The rider on the left has his helmet and his head back too far

Handlebar Positioning

Modifications can also be made to alleviate neck pain. A forty-five-degree angle in your back and a slight bend in your elbows indicate proper forward lean. (See photo on page 68.) Look down. The handle-bars should block the view of the front axle when you are sitting on your bike. This can be altered with height adjustments in the handlebar post, or by installing a different sized stem. Get your bike shop to help you with the fit -- they may have a spare stem out back that is just right for you.

Adjusting the height of the handlebar post

Stretching before, during and after the ride will also lessen some of the tension in your neck. Neck stretches can be done by slowly rotating your head in circles — just keep your eyes on the road!

Naturally, these adjustments are just suggestions since comfort varies from person to person. Most bicycle dealers will help you buy a bike that best fits your body or if it's too late for that, they will make adjustments with new parts. It's definitely worth the time, effort and money to take your bike to a reputable bike shop for a proper fit.

Hands

Another unpleasant result of long distance riding is hand pain and numbness. Hands get tender and bruised just like seats do and while there are padded bike gloves and handlebar tapes, it is yet another affliction that is often unavoidable. This is the result of bruised ulnar and median nerves, which supply feeling and strength to your hands.

The median nerve lies in the carpal tunnel and provides sensation to the thumb, index, middle and ring fingers. It also sends a motor branch to the muscles, which control thumb positioning. The ulnar nerve provides sensation to the ring and small fingers and controls the small muscles of the hand. The way to avoid hand numbness is simple – change hand positions frequently and keep a loose grip on the handlebars. Every so often, I simply let go of the handlebar grip and shake my hand from the wrist to keep it relaxed and loose.

Keep your weight on the seat and off the arms. Sustained compression and tight grasping are the major causes of hand numbness. A benefit to having down-turned handlebars that you find on road bikes is that you can change your hand positions, thus relieving pressure on certain parts of your hands. (Note the padded touring handlebars on the previous page's photo.) Though mountain bike handlebars are mostly straight, you can get end extensions, which give you adjustment options, too. Some riders use aerobar extensions on their handlebars to keep the weight off their palms altogether and change the position of their lower backs. No matter what type of handlebar you have, you must be sure to change your grip position regularly.

Posture

Many riders make the mistake of allowing their bones to support their upper bodies instead of their muscles, which can cause discomfort or injury from the shock of road bumps. Poor posture can affect the neck, back, hands, wrists and shoulders.

Poor riding posture

Proper riding posture

Adjustments to the back, shoulders and elbows can be made to ensure proper posture. In order to act as a shock absorber, the back should be arched, not sagging, and the elbows slightly bent. The shoulders should be pushed forward so that the chest muscles can help carry the weight of the upper body. Riders tend to let their bones support their upper body because it causes less muscle fatigue, but continuing to use good posture will eventually eliminate this fatigue and reduce other discomforts resulting from poor body positioning.

Stretching

Tight muscles hurt more and perform less efficiently. They also are more prone to injury. The more you strive to prevent muscle tightness, the better off you will be. Stretching regularly before, during and after your ride will help attain and maintain flexibility in your muscles and joints. Your stretching regimen should include your neck, legs, back, torso, and knees.

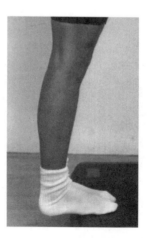

Achilles tendon stretch

Calf stretch

Lower back stretch

Lower back inner thigh stretch

There are a series of on-the-bike stretching exercises you can do to relieve some of the discomfort. First, drop your chin to your chest and roll it around gently to relieve stress on your neck. Next, bring one arm behind your back to stretch out your shoulder and chest, and complete a few arm circles. Repeat on the other side. Then, do a few shoulder shrugs. For your legs, frequently stand in the pedals and drop your heels to stretch your calves and tendons. If you do these every half-hour while riding you will not only feel better during the ride, you'll be ready to go again tomorrow.

5 / The Bicycle

There are four basic types of bicycles used for touring: touring bikes, mountain bikes, road bikes, and hybrids. If you are in the market for a new bike and plan to do a lot of touring, a touring bike is a worthwhile investment. If, however, you are not ready to spend any money it may be possible to use the bike you already have. We will discuss the benefits and limitations of all styles of bike in this chapter.

Touring bikes are designed for long distance riding

Your choice in a bicycle will involve many factors, not the least of which is personal preference. Try some bikes out and get one that fits your body and your pocketbook. If you already have a bike, see what needs to be done to make it ready for touring. We will walk you through some options and offer some suggestions.

The Touring Bike

Some years ago, before the advent of mountain biking, touring was a more popular pastime. All bike manufacturers produced special touring bikes and some even had a number of models in varying price ranges. After a period of relative obscurity, touring bikes have made a comeback, so there are many more options from which to choose.

Where To Find It:
Touring Bike Manufacturers

Bianchi	Bruce Gordon Cycles	Raleigh
(510) 264-1001	(707) 762-5601	(800) 222-5527
www.bianchi.it	www.bgcycles.com	www.raleighusa.com

Cannondale	Fuji	Rivendell Bicycle Works
(800) 245-3872	(800) 631-8474	(925) 933-7304
www.cannondale.com	www.fujibike.com	rivendellbicycles.com

Terry Precision Cycling	Trek	REI
(800) 289-8379	(800) 369-TREK	(888) 873-1938
www.terrybicycles.com	www.trekbikes.com	www.rei.com

Bikes made specifically for touring differ from road bikes in a number of ways. While they both feature drop handlebars, there is a slightly more upright riding position on a touring bike to aid comfort and maneuverability. They always have triple chainrings, giving up to 27 speeds. The frame has a longer chainstay so the rider's heels do not bump into the rear panniers. The wheel rims are stronger and thicker and tires wider. Cantilever brakes and greater frame clearance give space for fat tires and fenders, and welded on attachment points called braze-ons allow you to attach racks and multiple water bottles to the frame.

A touring bike loaded and ready to go

The Mountain Bike

The term 'mountain bike' is generic for a bike that is made to withstand the rigors of off-road riding. Some riders like the handlebars in the more upright seating position. They are more confident because of the bike's wider track and gladly give up a little speed for peace of mind. However, keep in mind that there are different types of mountain bikes today: one is not at all suited to touring, while the other is adaptable. The first type, called a 'full-suspension' or 'dualie,' has suspension on the front and rear of the bike, making it impossible to carry any kind of panniers. Such a bike is also difficult to ride long distances due to its 'squishy' feel. You tend to spend more time bouncing than moving forward.

A dual-suspension (dualie) mountain bike

A front-suspension (hard-tail) mountain bike

The second type of mountain bike, known as a 'hard-tail', has suspension on the front forks. Its major drawback is the inability to attach pannier racks to these forks. Such a bike can be used if you are carrying your load in a trailer, or are part of a tour that supplies SAG wagons. The best mountain bike option is one that has no suspension at all, as it is possible to attach carrying racks to the frame.

A road bike with handlebar extensions

The Road Bike

Road bikes aren't generally suited for touring due to the weight that they will be carrying, which they weren't really built to withstand. While your road bike might survive a few fully loaded tours, it will not last as long as a sturdier mountain or touring bike.

I didn't have the resources to buy a new bike for my West Coast tour, so I rode my Raleigh Supercourse aluminum frame road bike. Laurel stuck with her older model Trek racer after having a new freewheel and chain ring added to increase the gearing from twelve to twenty-one. Both bikes worked beautifully, which is really a tribute to the manufacturers because given the composition of the frames, they should not have been able to withstand the weight and rigors of the trip. With what I have since learned about bicycles since, I would say we were pretty lucky.

As with the suspension mountain bike, the road bike will work fine if you are carrying your gear in a cart or have the assistance of a SAG wagon.

The Hybrid Bike

The hybrid or commuting bikes that are on the market today are probably better suited to touring than the mountain or road bike. They have a slightly sturdier frame construction than a road bike, but less bulk than a mountain bike, making the weight less of a factor. The upright sitting position might also appeal more to some riders.

Many touring companies offer hybrids for short treks

Frame Material

Today's bicycles are made from a variety of materials including aluminum, steel, titanium, and carbon fiber. If you are going to buy a new bike, it is helpful to have a working knowledge about the differences in these materials.

A steel-framed hybrid is great for short tours

Stiffness, strength and weight are the three properties that will concern you when shopping for a bike. Stiffness refers to the amount of flexibility a frame has when forced to bend so that it springs back to its original position. The degree of stiffness in a frame affects how the bike feels to ride. Strength refers to the amount of force a frame can take before bending permanently. The degree of strength of a material will determine how durable a frame is or how it holds up to crashes, but has no influence on how it feels to ride. The weight of your bike is directly related to the material used to build the frame and the thickness of the tube wall. Obviously the most desirable frame would be one that is strong without being too heavy. As you might expect, the newer lighter frames cost more than heavier steel frames. The investment might be worth it if you're planning some long treks in hilly country.

Steel frames are the heaviest, the strongest, and the stiffest. Many riders prefer a stiff frame as it tends to feel more solid and absorb road shock a bit better than others. If you are more concerned about the weight of your frame, aluminum and titanium frames are preferable, but the compromise lies in strength and stiffness. Carbon fiber tubing is a relatively new technology, which gives strength and lightness, but its durability over long hauls is a question.

Much more technical explanations of frame materials are available, but probably not needed by an ordinary bicycling enthusiast. As I have suggested before, perhaps the best way to choose a suitable frame material when buying a bike is to take a few on test rides. Different frames have different feels and one might be more suited to you than another.

Bike Fit

Many of us do not have the luxury to buy a custom built bike, but that does not mean that we have to buy one that is poorly fitted. While certain adjustments can be made to the components to customize the fit of your bicycle, you really should start with a good frame fit. A number of years ago, the best way to test the fit of your bike was to stand over the top tube— if there was an inch of clearance between the tube and your crotch, the bike was considered a good fit. Nowadays there are many more styles and sizes of bikes to choose from, so the old method of sizing is no longer as effective.

Most reputable bike shop technicians will spend time trying to find a properly fitted bike for its customers, but if you are looking for complete accuracy, here are a few options.

1. If you are interested in buying a frame sized just for you,

go to a shop that makes custom frames and have them take your measurements using their fitting frame. They will take several hours to not only take measurements, but discuss your cycling plans and check your technique. The frame they build will be pricey but "yours."

2. Go to a shop that uses the FitKit, a system that measures your body in order to find the best bike fit. Many more shops are using the FitKit these days to meet the needs of their customers and while it is not really sensible to buy one yourself, you can call the company to find out what bike store in your area is using the technology.

Where To Find It
The FitKit System

FitKit Systems
Telephone/Fax: 406-248-6334
http://www.bikefitkit.com

3. Go on-line to any of the sites that explain in detail how to fit your bike. Some of these services are free and some will charge you a modest fee to determine the proper size bike for you.

Where To Find It
On-Line Bike Fit Instructions

Colorado Cyclist
http://www.coloradocyclist.com/BikeFit/index.cfm

B and J Bicycle Shop
http://www.bjbicycle.com/biofit/

Bicycles for Women

Until recently, the only difference between a men's bicycle and a women's bicycle was the absence of the top tube running from the seat to the handlebars. Women's bicycles were designed this way, originally, so that women could ride while wearing a skirt. Though such bikes can still be found on the market, any woman who plans to ride more than a mile at a time should not ride a bike without a top tube.

Women's bodies are built differently than men's, however, so adding a top tube is not enough. In recent years, women have become more serious about riding, both competitively and casually, so bicycle manufacturers are making bikes to suit them. One of the first companies to build bikes solely for women was Terry Precision Bicycling, started by Georgena Terry, an avid life-long bicycling enthusiast. Since her lead, other companies have followed suit, such as Specialized, Santa Cruz, Bianchi, Cannondale, Trek, and Gary Fisher. You can ask your local dealer for one of these in a woman's model or go on-line.

A quality bike shop will steer you to the right women's bike

**Where To Find It
Women's Bicycles**

Bianchi
Road Model
http://www.bianchi.it

Cannondale
Road Models
http://www.cannondalebikes.com

Gary Fisher
Mountain Models
http://www.fisherbikes.com

Specialized
Mountain Model
http://the-s-store.specialized.com

Terry Precision Cycling
Road Models
http://www.terrybicycles.com
Trek

Road Models
Mountain Models
http://www.trekbikes.com

I like to buy my bicycle and major equipment from a quality bike shop. When I'm out in the middle of nowhere, it's comforting to know that I'm aboard a well-tuned bike that fits me properly. I'm willing to pay a bit more to get the performance and reliability of a bicycle that will get me to the next campground, and home, safely.

6 / Outfitting the Bike and the Rider

Bike touring is one of the least expensive ways to travel. The biggest expense is the initial purchase of your gear which can run up to several thousand dollars. However, once you have your gear, you are all set for future trips. And there are ways to defray some of the initial costs. Some people go touring once and then never again and their gear collects dust in the basement. You might acquire such equipment through want ads or at sporting good consignment shops. There are also second-hand sports equipment sales at bike shops, schools, and town squares. You can also rent nearly all the non-cycling gear you will need from outdoor sporting good stores. Many stores will allow you to apply some of the rental fee toward the purchase price.

Share gear with a friend to cut costs and load

If you are riding with a friend, you can split some of the expenses. For instance, one of you can buy the cooking gear and stove and one can buy the tent. This not only cuts the cost, it cuts down on the load you have to carry. If you plan to do a lot of touring, you should purchase your own equipment, but before making that investment you might want to go on your first tour with borrowed gear. You might find that you want to sleep in motels and eat in restaurants.

Outfitting Your Bike

You will need to outfit your bike with the following equipment:

-bottle cages
-bungee cords
-cycle computer
-cycle computer battery
-front and rear pannier racks and bags or trailer
-handlebar bag
-lock
-mirror
-rear light (front, if planning to travel at night)
-tire
-tire pump or CO2 cartridge and inflator
-toe-clips or clipless pedals
-tools
-tubes
-water bottles (2 or more)

First, you need to carry your gear. Most people use pannier racks and bags, but gaining popularity in recent years are cargo carts that can be attached to the bike and hauled along behind.

Proponents of trailer use say that trailers give a better performance in headwinds and crosswinds, are easier to load and unload, stabilize the bike when riding, support the bike like a kickstand when parked, and make it possible to tour with a bike that won't accept panniers (like suspension bikes.)

Where To Find It
Trailers

B.O.B. Trailers   Colorado PackRack
(800) 893-2447   (303)670-2399
www.bobtrailers.com

RIO Watertight Trailers
(800) 357-2773
www.rio.com/~bsi/brev

Pannier fans prefer them for the following reasons:

1. they make it easier to park a bike in smaller areas,
2. they take up less space in campsites,
3. trailers have one more tire that can go flat (hence requiring you to lug along different sized tubes),
4. it is easier to keep things organized and accessible in panniers,
5. panniers and racks hold more gear than trailers, and they are easier to transport on airplanes.

Again, the use of trailers or panniers is a matter of personal preference but if you're just getting started, I recommend panniers.

A rear pannier

A front pannier

There are many kinds of panniers on the market from which to choose and though they may differ slightly in style, they all serve the same purpose — to distribute weight evenly over the wheels and keep your gear protected.

A loaded touring bike

There are also all types of smaller bags designed to fit various parts of your bike. I recommend that you also get a small handlebar bag which will give you easier access to items you need while riding. I love mine. If I had to get off my bike and search through bags every time I need to munch on a Powerbar, blow my nose, or coat my lips with Chapstick, I would never make it to my destination.

A handlebar bag

Rain covers are available for pannier bags, but if you don't want to spend the money, wrapping your gear in garbage bags before stuffing it in panniers works just as well.

You will, of course, need a lock. U-locks are great, but are rather heavy. I find that I never leave my bike alone long enough to require that much security, and if I did I would have to worry about my gear as well. So, a regular cable lock serves the purpose — usually only to lock the bike up at night. An advantage to riding with a partner is that when you have to go grocery shopping or leave your bikes alone in a high-risk area, one person is always there to guard them.

Two or more large water bottles and bottle cages are essential. Some bikes have fittings for three bottle cages, but I find that you can stop often enough for refills when needed. Some people are opting to use hydropacks, products designed to carry water in a pouch on your back, with a tube that runs to your mouth. The benefit of these is that you can drink without removing your hands from the bars to grab a bottle, therefore encouraging you to drink more often. The downside is that you have to carry something on your back, which might be uncomfortable or create more sweat. Whichever product you choose, make sure you have plenty of water at hand.

A hydropack allows you to drink "hands-free"

So, what else will you need? Well, obviously, spare tubes, tire changing irons and a pump. You can also carry tire-patching kits, if you are adept enough to use them. I tried it a few times and either could not find the puncture or could not get the patch to stick, so I gave up.

The downside of this incompetence is that we had to carry a lot of spare tubes as we got a lot of flat tires. I now carry tubes but also a patch kit, just in case I need it. (One benefit to mountain bikes and hybrids — their fatter tires are less apt to puncture.)

Tire changing equipment — patch kit, levers, pump, CO2 cartridge, tube

You will also need to carry some tools, but this will be covered in more detail in the chapter on bike maintenance. Again, if you're traveling with friends, split up the tool load. I suggest that you consider purchasing a multi-tool kit, of which there are many good ones, but be sure they have the right types of tools. We have included examples of multi-purpose tools on the following page.

Toe clips are a personal preference. Some people do not like having their feet strapped to their pedals, but most experienced riders rely on them to get maximum leg performance while pedaling. Some tourers opt for clipless pedals and shoes, which increase pedaling efficiency even more, and may also ease knee strain. But if you do buy clipless pedals, be sure to practice with them first. I have seen many a rider come to a complete stop before releasing their feet from the pedals, only to topple over on the pavement. There are bike shoes available that allow a rider to use clipless pedals which are also designed for easy walking.

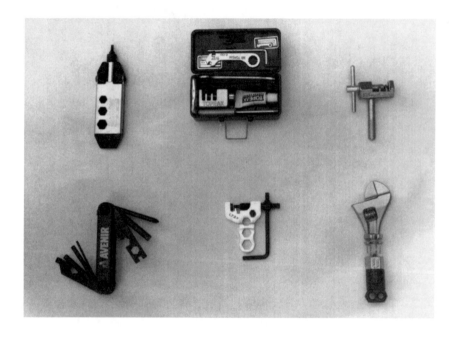

An assortment of multi-tools

I was hesitant to buy a pair of clipless pedals but a friend who was a rookie at biking, talked me into it. Karen was not a bike geek as a child and rarely rode as an adult, but after seeing the tail end of one of the Boston to New York AIDS Rides, she decided to sign up. She went out and bought a bike, all the gear, the outfits and the magazines, and became a bike fanatic nearly overnight. She even had clipless pedals. I shook my head and warned her, "Be careful, now. It is easy to fall off with those. Especially when trying to maneuver amongst

Clipless pedal

3000 other riders." While I was trying to sound concerned, I am sure I sounded condescending. The reality of it was that I was jealous. Here she was, the new kid, with clipless pedals, and I, the experienced rider, was too chicken to use them. Of course, she saw through all of my bluster and eventually convinced me to get a pair. I promised to wait until we could ride together before I tried them out so that she could witness me falling off my bike just as I had witnessed her, but I cheated and went out on my own.

Miraculously, I have not fallen yet. It is simply a matter of remembering that your feet are clipped in before you come to a stop so you can release them. Being paranoid about falling, I am constantly aware of this fact. I'm sure I will fall off sooner or later — hopefully while riding with Karen so she can get a chuckle — but even with that imminent possibility, the pedals truly are worthwhile. Now, I often wonder how I ever got along without them.

Cycle computers have replaced the odometers of old, and today offer a number of options. Despite my inability to set the clock on my VCR, I have managed to decipher the instructions on my cycle computer. My computer offers the following functions:

-speed

-average speed

-trip distance

-overall distance

-cadence

-time

Less expensive ones only offer speed, distance, and time, which would actually be enough for me. All I ever really needed to know was how far I'd gone, how fast I was moving, and how long it was taking me to get there. The rest was irrelevant.

Drop handlebars and cycling computer

The mirror that I purchased en route on my first major tour was my best investment of the trip. When riding a fully loaded bike it is difficult, if not dangerous, to turn and look behind you every time you sense an oncoming vehicle. Your balance is far too precarious as it is. With a mirror, you can keep an eye on things with ease. It is also a great way to keep track of your riding partner. While there are mirrors that can be attached to sunglasses or helmets, I prefer the handlebar mirror. I have tried the other two and have found the mirrors to be too small, difficult to keep adjusted, and prone to breaking when laying my helmet down. Handlebar mirrors will fit different types of handlebars and are relatively sturdy, and easy to adjust.

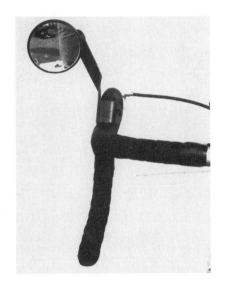
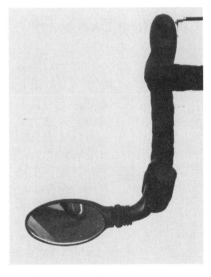

Two options for mounting handlebar mirrors

I have never brought a bike light on tour since I've had no intention to ride at night, but if you do, there are a number of powerful lights on the market, ranging from the more powerful, longer-lasting and more expensive ones, to smaller, less powerful, cheaper ones.

Where To Find It
Bike Lights

Night Sun
http://www.night-sun.com

Bike Lights
http://www.iawathletics.com

Bike Nashbar
(800) NASHBAR
http://www.nashbar.com

Colorado Cyclist
(800) 688-8600
http://www.coloradocyclist.com

Performance Bicycle Shop
http://www.performancebike.com

Pricepoint
(800) 774-2376
http://www.pricepoint.com

Outfitting The Biker

That pretty much covers it for the bike, now what about the biker? Some of the things you will need:

-helmet
-sunglasses
-padded gloves
-biking shoes
-biking shorts
-rain gear
-bandanas
-space blanket

Of course, you will wear a helmet, right? Right. As you tour, you will encounter long-distance riders who forgo helmets and who will ride with headsets playing their favorite tunes. I hope they hear that RV coming up behind them. I too never wore a helmet until I went on my first tour and even then I hesitated for the sake of vanity. I learned quickly that with or without a helmet my hairstyle was going to be shot, so I may as well opt for safety. Buy a good helmet from a bike shop and get it fitted to you. Your chin strap should be tight and the helmet snug but comfortable. The other benefit to helmets is that they are a great place to put souvenir stickers.

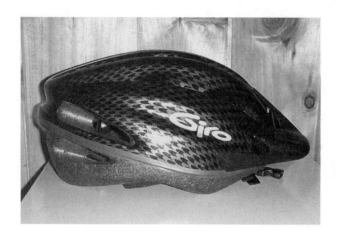

Invest in a good helmet — and wear it

Sunglasses are critical to protect your eyes from sun, debris and wind. After years of wearing cheap, drugstore-purchased shades, I finally bought a pair of expensive glasses with good lenses. What a difference they make. A good lens will make visibility much better and cut down on eyestrain and fatigue. They really are worth the money. Some manufacturers make bicycling glasses that have interchangeable lenses for different types of light conditions.

Make sure to wear padded gloves which will ease the pressure on your palms and help protect from road rash in case you take a spill.

If using clipless pedals, you will have to wear cleated bike shoes. Nowadays, these come in racing, ATB, and touring styles, and range from truly ugly to pretty cool looking. If you are using toe clips or just pedals, try a sport shoe with a firm sole — check with your bike shop for recommendations. Don't try to pedal long distances in running shoes, they're too flexible. I also bring Tevas to wander around camp at night.

A biking shoe that can be used with toe clips or clipless pedals

Biking shorts are another critical item, as discussed earlier. They vary from sleek Lycra to baggy shorts with pockets. I carry three to four pairs, which serve me fairly well between laundry days. Rain gear of some sort is also a must, though I'm not sure there is any raingear that will keep you totally dry. At one point, I had a special biking rainsuit, which was lightweight and breathable, but not even remotely waterproof. I have since replaced it with a rain/wind suit that has an inside layer as well, which seems to keep me a bit drier. There is also more expensive rain gear on the market which is probably the best defense against wetness. Rainsuits serve nicely as cold weather gear, too. You have to come to terms with the fact that no matter how much you spend on rain gear, when riding in the rain you will get wet. It's all part of the bargain. As an added note, when buying rain gear be sure it is a bright color. You will need the visibility in foul weather riding.

Pick rain gear in bright colors

I did make a valuable discovery during one of the Boston to New York AIDS Rides. On two of the Rides, we ended up riding through the tail ends of hurricanes. It was cold, we were beyond wet, and many people were being carted away to hospitals for hypothermia. Luckily, the Ride staff was handing out silver Mylar sheets that were leftover from the Boston Marathon. My friend, Kathy, and I grabbed a bunch of these and wrapped them around our bodies, under our already soaked clothes. They helped keep some of the heat in. The problem with Mylar, however, is that it tears easily, so I would suggest buying a few of these and maybe even a thicker Space Blanket, which you can buy from any camping store. I'm sure it would have many other uses, too.

The other indispensable item is the bandana. They have a million uses, from checking flat tires for nails to warding off black flies.

Cell Phones and GPS Units

At the time of my first tour, cell phones were just coming onto the market. Neither Laurel nor I had one, and in retrospect, it would have been very helpful if we did. A cell phone can help you find out the availability of campsites ahead of time, or notify authorities in case of an emergency. I never ride without my cell phone now, whether I am in the woods or on the road.

Keep your eye on global positioning system (GPS) units. Relying on satellites, these compact units can give you your exact position on a map display as well as the distance to your next checkpoint. They are coming down in size and price. Hikers, canoeists, aviators, and many others are using compact handheld units. You can share your trips with others through the Internet and download maps and directions. With a moving map display and ground speed readout, you may soon be able to toss your maps (well, better keep your maps in the pannier — along with the spare GPS batteries.)

Personal Gear

One thing annoying about biking/camping/traveling guidebooks is that they tell you what clothes to bring on a trip. Now, how is someone going to tell me how many pairs of underwear I should bring? A general rule of thumb is bring enough clothing to keep comfortable, but pack as light as you can. Face it, your clothes will get dirty and smelly and you won't be able to get to a Laundromat as often as you would like to. It's OK. Everyone else is dirty and smelly.

For comfort sake, I reserve a pair of shorts and a T-shirt for campsite and sleepwear and I only put those on after showering. This way I feel relatively fresh and clean at night. Then I have my biking clothes, which I will wear again and again. I'd suggest that you not bring your favorite t-shirts, because they will get trashed beyond recognition by the trip's end. And if you can't stand to wear that filthy, stained shirt one more time, you can always toss it and buy a new one.

Some folks wear fancy Lycra or Capilene biking shirts. These are designed to dry quickly when perspiring and therefore keep you from getting chilled. They also have pockets in the back for carrying snacks. It's up to you whether or not you want to look like a "pro." In any case, do explore some of the new outdoor wear materials. What works for hikers and climbers may be just what keeps you warm and dry when that squall line arrives unexpectedly.

Don't forget socks and the appropriate warm weather gear for colder climes. Nothing will make you more miserable, or put you in more danger, than being cold. I bring a Polartec fleece jacket and pants on my trip, which keep me warm enough at camp at night and as a layer as needed by day. Be sure to research the weather trends where you are touring so you can pack accordingly.

If it sounds like I pack the perfect types and amounts of clothes for my trips, don't be misled. During my first tour, Laurel and I shipped home a box full of unneeded gear, including sundresses and sandals. What, pray tell, were we thinking? It was a bike tour, not a garden party. If you have extra clothes that you can bear to part with, you can always leave them behind in a campground restroom with a note saying they are free to a good home. You never know, another biker, tired of his or her wardrobe, just might snatch them up.

Other personal items I found necessary were my journal, which I never go anywhere without, a book, stamps, envelopes, pens, camera, film, and my address/phone book. A deck of cards is also a fun idea.

As for toiletries, if you are traveling with a friend, you can share some of these items and therefore cut down on weight and space. Again, these items are personal so I can't tell you what to bring. I will inform you, however, that a curling iron and back brush are probably not necessary. And, oh yeah, don't forget a towel. The smaller, the better, as it will dry more quickly and take up less valuable space. Terrycloth does not dry quickly, especially when stuffed in pannier bags. There are small, packable towels on the market now that soak up a lot of water and dry quickly. They are a worthwhile investment.

A first aid kit is also an important addition. You can either buy a pre-packaged kit, or make your own. It should include:

- –Ace Bandage
- –Antacid/Anti-gas tablets
- –Anti-bacterial ointment
- –Antiseptic wipes
- –Antihistamine tablets
- –Anti-itch creme
- –Aspirin
- –Band-Aids/Bandages (various sizes)
- –Eye drops
- –Insect repellent
- –Lip balm
- –Matches
- –Medical Adhesive Tape
- –Moleskin
- –Mylar sheet/Space Blanket
- –Needle and thread
- –Prescription medications
- –Protective Gloves
- –Safety Pins
- –Sunblock
- –Tweezers
- –Vaseline

Camping Gear

There's still more. Here are some items you will need if you are not staying in motels or hostels:

         –clothespins
         –flashlight
         –groundcloth
         –headlamp (to work in the dark with your hands free)
         –knife
         –matches
         –plastic bags (large and small)
         –rope
         –sleeping bag
         –sleeping pad
         –spare batteries
         –string
         –tent
         –tent stakes

These items should be as light and compact as possible.

Cooking on a gas stove

Cooking Gear

The amount of cooking gear you bring depends on the type of cooking you plan to do. Generally, you will need the following items.

- bandana
- bowl
- camp stove
- cooking pot (Teflon is easier to clean)
- cup
- eating utensils
- fuel for stove
- knife
- matches
- nylon scrub pad
- small container of dish soap
- wooden cooking spoon

Packing Your Bike

Now then, how in the world will all that stuff fit on a bike? There are a few technical rules for loading your bike:

1. Always use both front and rear panniers. Some people are able to load all of their gear onto the backs of their bikes, but this is a giant mistake, making handling and maneuverability severely limited.
2. Distribute the weight evenly on each side or you will spend your days riding like the Leaning Tower of Pisa (which is as bad for your mood as it is for your spokes.)
3. Distribute the gear between the front and rear of the bike so that approximately 2/3 of the weight is in the front. This will make handling easier.
4. Carry the heaviest weight low and close to the frame.

If you are riding alone the packing job gets pretty tricky. Thilo was alone on his three-month tour and his bike resembled the car in which the Beverly Hillbillies crossed the United States. All that was missing was the rocking chair. But if you are riding with a partner, you can divide some of the stuff between you. You carry the cooking gear and have your friend carry the tent. Easy enough.

Obviously, you will want the things you need to get at during the day at close reach, like in your handlebar bag. The sleeping bag and pad, and the tent are loaded on top of your rear rack. This is where bungee cords of all shapes and sizes are needed. Of course, as time goes on, you will pack your loads again and again, finally perfecting the system. It is my answer to house cleaning while on the road; not that I ever miss that activity. And again, if you are accumulating things that you do not need (souvenirs, gifts), stop at a post office and send them home.

7 / Bicycle Repair and Maintenance

There is a vast collection of books on the shelf in your local bookstore on bicycle repair and maintenance. My advice, however, is don't carry one with you and don't expect to know what to do unless you've already tried. Bike maintenance is not something one learns solely from reading a manual; it is a skill acquired through tinkering with bikes, taking them apart, putting them together, making mistakes and correcting them. The books are helpful, mind you, they just should not be your only resource if you are not already familiar with the process. While it is not imperative to know bike repair and maintenance to go on a tour, if you're not on a van-support tour, it is a good idea to become familiar with your bike. If you get comfortable with some simple maintenance and repair techniques, you will not only save money by keeping the bike running well but, when you're stuck beside a rural road, it might just get you to your next campground. A little knowledge, coupled with a little practice before you head out, is all that you need. The more you ride, the more you will learn about fixing bikes. Repairing bicycles has been a hobby of mine since getting my first ten-speed bicycle for my thirteenth birthday. I still remember every detail of that bike. It was a cherry red Concorde with yellow labels and handlebar tape; it had a Simplex derailleur and Mavic center pull brakes (those were hot items in those days.) It cost $105, which was a fair amount of money then.

My best childhood friend, Amey, and I spent more time disassembling our bikes than riding them in those days. She had a bright orange Atala and loved it as much as I loved mine. We both asked our fathers for a corner of the garage to set up "bike stations." For some reason, our young minds believed that it was not good for the wheels to be resting on the ground all of the time, so we built towel covered racks (didn't want any scratches!) to hold them up. We made shelves for tools and gear and our "bike stations" became the only tidy oases in otherwise disorganized garages. I don't really know how we got so interested in our bikes, but the fascination has continued.

Since then, I have repaired, overhauled and repainted all types of bikes in all kinds of conditions. I always have a how-to manual by my side, but mostly I learn by doing. I recently overhauled my mountain bike. Bike technology changes with each passing year, so many of the components, I found, were new to me. After taking my bike apart completely, I laid the many pieces out on the floor. A friend who was visiting asked if I knew what I was doing. "Honestly?" I answered. "No. But I will figure it out." She looked at me skeptically and I assured her that if I couldn't get it back together correctly, I would take it to my bike shop and let them do it for me. I did, in fact, get it all back together, but I did take it to my bike mechanic for fine-tuning of the gears. The good thing about tinkering with a bike is that if something goes amiss on a tour, you'll know how to correct it.

Pre-Ride Overhaul

If you are unable to do it yourself, I would strongly suggest that you have a bike shop give your bike an overhaul/tune up before you go on your trip. Tires need to be checked for wear, brake pads should be replaced, rusty or frayed cables should be changed, and the derailleurs and brakes probably need adjustment. You should also do a bearing check on the headset, bottom bracket, and hubs, and all moving parts should be cleaned and lubricated.

Tools and Spare Parts

I have collected tools over the years from area bike shops and mail order companies. As shown last chapter, there are great mini-tool kits that have nearly everything a biker needs for on-the-road repairs. They are small, compact, and weigh a lot less than standard tools. They are a worthwhile investment.

It is important to carry tools on a tour even if you aren't well versed in bicycle maintenance. The tools and replacement parts you should carry with you are:

- adjustable crescent wrench
- bike grease
- brake pads
- cables — brake and gear
- chain links
- chain remover
- citrus gel
- duct tape
- lubricant
- multiple Allen wrench
- multiple screwdriver kit
- presta valve adapter
- rack mounting bolts and hooks
- spokes & spoke wrench
- surgical gloves
- Swiss Army knife
- third hand brake tool
- tire & tubes
- tire irons
- tire patching kit
- tire pressure gauge
- zip ties

It is a good idea to oil your chain and gear components every 200 miles to keep things rolling smoothly. Teflon spray is a product on the market that lubricates parts without leaving an oily build-up. Do not use motor oil, mineral oil, household oil such as 3-in-1 or WD-40, or bearing grease to lubricate your components. A small tube of bike grease is handy for repacking bearings. I like to bring a few pairs of rubber surgical gloves so my hands don't get too grimy when doing messier jobs, but I also carry small packets of citrus gel which cleans bike grease from your skin like magic, doesn't smell nasty, and leaves your hands feeling soft. It's one of the great advances of science. You can get this from bike stores or local hardware and auto mechanic shops. Granted, you may never have to use any of these items, but it's nice to have them if you do.

Lubricate your chain and key components about every 300 kilometers

Important Basics to Know

While a pre-ride overhaul can be done by a bicycle shop, I would advise that you know some basic bike repair/maintenance before setting out on a tour, or at least ride with someone who does. You can try these things at home before you go, and if you still lack confidence, photocopy the pages of your bike repair book to take along with you. Some schools and bike shops offer continuing education classes where you might find a bike maintenance course. While fellow riders are usually happy to assist you with minor repairs, if you are alone in the middle of nowhere and something goes wrong, it's great to know some basic maintenance.

Changing Flat Tires

Even if you keep the tire pressure pumped up, your most common problem will be flat tires. Follow these simple guidelines for changing a flat tire:

    1. There is a release lever on your brake unit that will open up the brakes in order to remove the wheel with ease. Open this lever and remove the wheel.

Opening the brake release lever

2. Your tube will have one of two types of valve stems: Presta or Schraeder.

A Presta valve (left) and a Shrader valve (right)

3. Unscrew the valve cover first.

4. If the valve stem is Schraeder, depress the inner button to release remaining air. If it is a Presta, unscrew the top of the valve and push down to release air.

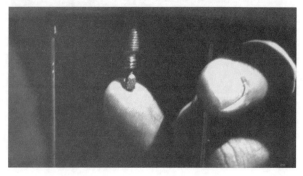

5. Insert the end of one tire lever under the tire edge and hook the other end to the spoke. Don't start near the valve.

6. Insert the second tire lever in a similar way a few inches from the first tire lever.

7. Use the third tire lever to slide the rest of the tire edge off one side of the rim. Leave other side of tire edge on the other rim.

8. Carefully remove the inner tube, inspect the inside of the tire, and remove any sharp objects that may have caused the flat by running your finger around the inside of the tire and rim. (Wrap a bandana around your finger.)

Remove the tube and then check the tire carefully with your finger

9. Make sure rubber strip on inside of the rim is straight and completely covering the tops of the spokes.

10. If you wish to replace your tube with a new one, skip to step 14. If you wish to patch your tube, locate the puncture by inflating the tube with your pump. Listen for escaping air. If you're near water, you can immerse the tube and watch for air bubbles.

11. After locating the puncture, wipe off the area with a rag. Rough up the area with sandpaper contained in your patch kit.

12. Apply rubber cement contained in your patch kit and let dry for 5 minutes.

13. Peel off the back of an adhesive tire patch and fasten the patch in place over the puncture.

14. Once more, check the outside of your tire for nails or other foreign objects and then run your bandana-wrapped finger around the inside of the tire to make sure there are no sharp pieces.

15. Remount the tube back in the tire. First, place the valve stem back through the rim hole, making sure it is straight. Tuck the rest of the tube inside the tire, working away from the valve.

16. Using your hands, reinstall the tire onto the rim. Do not use tire irons unless absolutely necessary as they might pinch and tear the deflated tube.

Use your hands to reinstall the tire onto the rim

17. If your valve stem is Schraeder style, you can inflate your tube with an ordinary pump. If it is Presta, you need a pump that has a Presta head or a Presta valve adapter. I personally like to keep Presta adapters on my tubes instead of protective covers to accommodate gas station or traditional pumps.

18. Inflate the tire part way and check that the tire edge is even all the way around the rim.

Inflate the tire part way and check that the tire edge is even

19. Finish inflating the tire to the pressure mark indicated on the sidewall. If you don't have a pressure gage, inflate so it's hard to the touch and then stop at the next gas station to top off or correct the pressure.
20. If you are using Presta valves, be sure to screw the top back down.
21. Remount the wheel on your bike, checking alignment and brake adjustment.
22. Make sure that you re-apply the brake release levers before you ride!!

This is simpler than it sounds. Don't wait to learn during a bike tour, practice at home with someone who's done it. If you tour, you'll get flats so fixing flats is a vital skill to master.

Replacing a Broken Chain

Chain repair requires the use of a chain tool, which drives the pin of the chain link almost out of the hole so that you can separate the links. To replace your chain, take these steps:

1. Attach your chain tool to any link.

2. Slowly turn the knob until the chain pin is pushed almost all of the way out. The resistance should increase as the end meets the pin wall. WARNING! Do not remove pin completely or you will not be able to replace it.

Using a chain tool

3. Unscrew turning knob and remove chain tool.

4. Hold chain on either side of removed pin and bend to separate it. If it won't separate, push pin out a little farther.

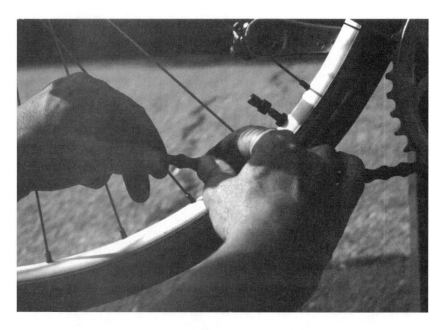

Hold chain on either side of removed pin and bend to separate it.
(Note the adaptor on the Presta valve stem)

Replacing the chain

5. Replace chain with new one.

6. Attach chain tool to open link and turn knob to push pin back in to link.

7. Gently grasp either side of newly applied link and bend back and forth to eliminate stiffness.

8. Lubricate chain thoroughly with a Teflon spray or other special lubricant that does not collect excess dirt.

Chains need to be cleaned regularly to ensure a smooth ride and extend the life of your drivetrain. Degreasing solvents can be purchased at a bike shop or on-line and chain-cleaning boxes are available to enable you to clean your chain without removing it completely. Do not use WD-40, 3 in 1 Oil or other non-bicycle specific lubricants. These only attract more grit and shorten the life of your chain and gears.

**What To Look For
Chain Cleaners and Lubricants**

–Pedro's Chain Lubes and Cleaners
–White Lightening Products
–Finish Line Lubes and Cleaners

Clean your chain regularly

Replacing Brake Pads

Most bicycles have one of three types of brakes: disk, side-pull, and cantilever. With brake and gear cables often running from the same levers on newer model bikes, and derailleurs being spring loaded, making adjustments is rather complicated. Anything beyond changing brake pads should be left to the experts at your local bike shop. Brake pad replacement, however, is quite simple.

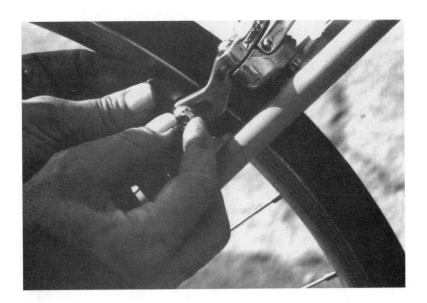

Replacing a brake pad

Brake pads wear out with usage, especially if you are riding in wet conditions. They should be changed regularly to ensure safe stopping. More expensive brake pads will last longer and give smoother, safer stops. When you purchase new pads make sure you get the right type of pad for the type of brake you have.

1. Loosen the brake pad holding nut and remove old pads.
2. Replace old pad with new one.

8 / Safety and Health

There is a wonderful book called *Miles From Nowhere*, which recounts the round-the-world journey of husband and wife, John and Barbara Savage. After years of bike travel, the Savages returned home safely to California. One day Barbara hopped on her bike to make a run to the corner store and, tragically, was struck by a car and killed. While such an incident may seem like fate, and perhaps it was, it points out that even the most seasoned rider can run into unexpected trouble. We will cover a few basics to help keep you safe and sound during your training and your touring.

Often, experienced riders are the most susceptible to danger. Comfortable on their bikes, they grow less vigilant about their actions. It is for this reason that the officials of the Boston to New York AIDS Rides give the bicycling veterans a more strident warning at the safety orientation. The underlying motto for all participants of the Ride is "Stay Alert, Stay Alive," and it should be the mantra for all riders on the road, whether on an organized ride or alone.

Riding in Traffic

Most motorists follow traffic rules. Traffic, therefore, can flow smoothly because drivers can predict what other drivers will do. Collisions usually occur when someone does something unpredictable.

When you ride a bike in traffic, you can maneuver better than the cars around you, so it is often tempting to ignore the traffic rules. Do not. When you break traffic laws you put yourself in danger: motorists and other cyclists will not know what you will do next, making it harder to avoid you and prevent a crash. However, if you act like a vehicle —signaling turns, turning from the correct lane, and stopping at lights, drivers can predict what you will do.

Being predictable is the key to safe riding in traffic.

Rules of the Road

1. Bicycles must adhere to the same traffic laws, signals and markings as autos. If you are unsure of these, read the "Rules of the Road" or a similar publication from your state's motor vehicle department.
2. Use hand signals to indicate turning and stopping. The left hand pointed to the left indicates a left turn, as shown below.

Right turn signal

You signal a right turn by bending your arm up at the elbow. The left hand bent down indicates that the rider is stopping or slowing.

3. Never ride against traffic. Despite the fact that it feels safer to see cars coming at you, it is not. A head-on collision with a car will have a much greater impact that one with a car that is moving with you.

4. Change lanes before turning left if traffic is moving slowly. Move into the lane farthest to the left when turning, if traffic is slow. If traffic is moving rapidly, wait for a gap and cross all lanes at once.

5. Do not pass on the side to which a car is turning.

Safe Riding Techniques

1. When riding, always consider yourself invisible to motorists. Never assume they can see you or know what your intentions are.
2. Always be wary of cars parked on the side of the street. Keep a look out for the possibility of drivers opening their doors.
3. Beware of obstructions: sand, gravel, potholes, and road grates.
4. Cross railroad tracks on a right angle.
5. When passing other cyclists or pedestrians, yell "on your left" to warn them.
6. When riding in the rain, use extra caution. Roads become slick as thin sheets of oil, gas and grease form on the surface. Fallen leaves become slippery during rains.
7. Brakes stop working when wet. When riding through puddles or in rain, pump your brakes periodically to dry them off.
8. Wear bright clothing to increase visibility.
9. Some riders carry a whistle to use in highly trafficked areas to warn motorists of their presence.
10. To avoid flying over the handlebars when stopping, never use the front brake alone. If back wheel starts to skid, it is a warning that you might take flight.
11. Always wear a helmet.

Riding the Loaded Bike

There are some technical aspects to consider when training for your bike tour. Most important is that you practice riding your loaded bike ahead of time. Neither Laurel nor I did for our first tour and it almost resulted in disaster.

When we first got on our loaded bikes, we were outside of our hotel in Seattle. The hotel sat atop a steep hill on a heavily trafficked street whose sides were chock full of parked cars. I climbed on my bike, stuck my foot into the toe clip, pushed off with the other, started rolling, and panicked. Within seconds, I was off the bike, a cold sweat encasing my body. Laurel had not mounted yet and looked at me with alarm.

"What's wrong?" she asked.

"I can't do it, Laurel. I can't ride my bike. I am going to fall over. We can't go."

She gave me a "you're-such-a-drama-queen" look and took off on her bike, only to stop within inches of me, eyes wide with shock. There we were on the first day of our trip and we couldn't even ride our bikes.

"Maybe we can get training wheels," I quipped.

Needless to say, there is a vast difference between riding a naked bike and riding one that is packed for tour. The balance is completely thrown off by the weight, the maneuverability is greatly reduced, and the stopping distance is considerably lengthened. And a hilly city street is not the best place to discover this. This is one of those things that you should definitely try at home.

Take your loaded bike on a "shakedown cruise"

To ride the loaded bike safely, follow these guidelines:

1. Remember that your bike is heavier and less maneuverable. Ride it with this in mind.
2. Don't pedal through steep turns because you are liable to catch a pedal on the road, which will cause a crash.
3. Due to the momentum of a heavier bike, your braking power is greatly reduced, so look ahead so that you have ample time to react to potholes, gravel, railroad tracks, and other road hazards.
4. Do not ride too fast since braking effectiveness is reduced.
5. Brake before going into turns, and if you have to brake, use rear brake only and squeeze lightly.
6. Never use the front brake alone.

The Shakedown Cruise

In addition to getting used to handling a bike loaded with gear, there's another reason to take some loaded rides before embarking on your journey. It's what boaters call a 'shakedown cruise.' They do this right before leaving on an extended cruise to ensure that everything is in working order. The same holds true for touring. You need to make sure your equipment works and your packs fit properly and are attached securely. These are not things to discover when stuck in the middle of nowhere.

Dogs

Although I love dogs, they can be scary when they approach barking and snarling. Generally, they are just trying to protect their territory, and if you do not make eye contact and move quickly out of their boundaries, they will leave you alone. If you can't outpedal a dog, stop cycling, keeping the frame between you and the animal — sometimes the rhythm of the wheels is causing the problem. I'm not shy about yelling sharply at canines, as I ease out of their territory.

I always carry a can of pepper spray in my handlebar bags. It is a good precaution if faced with aggressive dogs as well as unwelcome strangers. Fortunately, I haven't needed to use it, but having it makes me feel better. A well-aimed spray from a water bottle also works well on most dogs.

Health Precautions

While staying healthy during a bike tour largely depends on proper training, ample sleep and good nutrition, there a number of other potentially dangerous factors of which riders should be aware. Here are some of the important ones.

Dehydration

Never let yourself become dehydrated. It can kill you. To avoid dehydration, drink a lot of water throughout your ride. Start well before you are thirsty and keep at it. Sports drinks are helpful for replacing electrolytes and giving energy boosts, but water is the most important fluid for riders.

Perspiration acts as a coolant, pumping heat from your working muscles out to the skin where it can be released to the outside air. It is critical to replace that lost liquid with water and other fluids. Have you ever noticed that even though you have consumed plenty of liquids while perspiring, you still don't have to pee? That is because your body has absorbed the water that was lost and there is no waste to eliminate.

Easily recognizable signs of dehydration are sunken eyes, wrinkled skin, dry mouth and dark yellow urine.

Do not drink alcohol or caffeine-laden beverages. Both are diuretics which will make you urinate more and, therefore, cause further dehydration. The best bet is to drink water early and often during a long ride. An ounce of prevention...

Heat Exhaustion

Heat exhaustion occurs when someone is exposed to very hot weather, or a combination of heat and humidity, and does not take in adequate salt and water. As a result, the body can't get rid of the heat load placed on it. Excessive sweating causes water and salt loss as the body unsuccessfully tries to cool off. Your becomes pale and clammy. You may feel sick, dizzy and faint, your pulse rate and breathing may become rapid, and a headache and/or muscle cramps may develop.

If you think that you are experiencing heat exhaustion, lie down in a cool place with your feet slightly raised. Drink plenty of water and take some salt tablets.

Heatstroke

Heatstroke usually occurs after prolonged exposure to very hot conditions. The mechanism in the brain that normally regulates body temperature rises to 140. The person is confused or unconscious, and is flushed, with hot, dry skin and strong, rapid pulse. Heatstroke is a medical emergency and treatment should be sought immediately.

If you or a riding partner are experiencing heatstroke, immerse him/her in cool or tepid water and/or fan him/her by hand or with an electric fan. Continue this process until body temperature has dropped to at least 101 degrees or until help arrives.

Heatstroke and heat exhaustion can both be avoided by riding during the cooler hours of the day, drinking plenty of fluids and taking dips in rivers or lakes along the way.

Hypothermia

Hypothermia is just as deadly as heatstroke. During prolonged exposure to cold, more body heat may be lost than can be replaced, so body temperature may drop. Hypothermia occurs when the body temperature falls.

When the Titanic sunk, hundreds of passengers clung to life pre-servers in the Atlantic Ocean. Though the death certificates reported drowning, the real cause of death for most of the victims was hypo-thermia. The icy water drew heat and life out of the victims' bodies.

You don't have to be floating in cold water to get hypothermia. People have suffered hypothermia in 50-degree air. Be aware of the wind chill when cycling and stay warm enough. When chilling rain hits, put on your windbreaker or rain gear. Wear leg tights when it is below 68 degrees and long sleeves when the urge hits. Heat is lost through the extremities so wear warm gloves, ear covering, and shoe covers in colder weather.

Do not, on any account, wear cotton in wet weather. When cot-ton gets wet, it draws the heat out of your body. Wool, polypropylene and other man-made fibers that are used in sportswear are good in wet and dry weather alike.

You can tell a person is becoming hypothermic by his/her behav-ior. Because the decrease in body temperature causes gradual physi-cal and mental slowing, the affected person will become increasingly clumsy, unreasonable, and irritable. Speech may become slurred and the victim will become increasingly drowsy and confused. Without intervention, the person may go into a coma and have slow, weak breathing and heart rate. Emergency help should be sought, but until it arrives the following steps can be taken:

a)   If the person has stopped breathing, administer artificial res-piration.

b)   Once breathing is regular, shelter the person from the cold. If you have to remain outside, cover the person's head and insulate him/her from the ground to prevent further heat loss.

c)   If possible, dress the person in warm, dry clothes and give warm liquids to drink if he/she does not cough or vomit.

d)   Another person's body heat can help raise the temperature of a hypothermia victim. Lie closely to the affected person, holding him/her tight.

I have experienced the beginning of hypothermia while tubing down a local river. Though the temperature of the air was in the 80's and the sun was shining, the prolonged immersion in cold water made my body temperature drop considerably. It took hours for me to warm up, despite wrapping up in piles of clothes and sitting in a heated car. I felt the cold, it seemed, down in the cells of my body, and I shook uncontrollably for hours. It was a frightening and uncomfortable experience, one that I would hate to have while out in the middle of nowhere on a bike.

Rest

While on tour, listen to your body. This should not be difficult, as you will probably be more in tune with it than you normally are. If it feels overwhelmingly fatigued, stop for a day and rest. Your body is damaged by exercise. It is during the resting period that follows the exercise that it heals and gets stronger. Do not be so concerned with losing a day of riding that you lose an entire trip.

Safety and Self-Defense

Many people asked Laurel and I if we were afraid to be two women alone on a tour. The answer was always no. There were always other bikers at campgrounds and we assumed, being like-minded people, that they could be trusted. Whenever we rode long distances on desolate roads, we were too busy playing games to relieve the monotony to worry about anyone hurting us. I was so confident about my safety, in fact, that I would not hesitate to do a tour alone.

I may be naïve and perhaps I see the world through rose-colored glasses, as my friends say I do, but I really don't worry about such things. Granted, I try not to be foolish, but I generally believe that you can't hide from life.

If you listen to the alarmists, you will never venture out of your home. But you can take some sensible precautions. I always carry a can of pepper spray on my bike in an easy to reach place and whenever I am in the campground. I always camp at commercial sites, never just settling in a deserted field or spot in the woods. And, I avoid riding at night.

There are some common sense self-defense strategies with which all people, men and women alike, should be familiar. As a second-degree black belt in Tae Kwon Do, I have learned these tactics through years of training. They do not encompass fancy kicks and flips, but are simply things to think about. A simple awareness of these self-defense options can make a difference in your personal safety and self-confidence.

Avoidance

a) Do not put yourself in obviously risky situations. Clearly, it is wise to avoid the 'bad' side of town when in cities. Sticking to main routes should help you avoid this.

b) Avoid making eye contact with suspicious-looking individuals, or people who make you feel uncomfortable. Eye contact can create an unwanted connection or be perceived as aggression.

c) Be aware of what your body language projects. When walking or standing, hold yourself erect, keep your head up and eyes alert. This will prevent you from looking like a victim, and instead create an aura of self-confidence, strength, and purpose.

d) If someone is trying to rob you, give him/her whatever he/she wants, no matter what. Your safety is much more valuable than any object you own.

9/ Food

An athlete's body is like a car: in order to run properly, it needs the right type and amount of fuel. Some people rely on the expertise of sports nutritionists when training, but all you really need to do to start bike touring is make sure your diet is well balanced and that you compensate for the extra energy your body is expending.

The key to good nutrition while bicycling is to eat before you are hungry and drink before you are thirsty. Complex carbohydrates are the best source of fuel for your muscles. These include pasta, beans, rice, whole grains, fruits and vegetables. Ideally, your diet should be composed of the following:

> 60% carbohydrates
> 20% protein
> 20% fat
> plenty of water

New research warns against restricting fat in your diet as many health-conscious athletes and vegetarians tend to do. While lowering fat intake may reduce cholesterol, it also deprives the body of protein, iron, zinc and calcium. Fat is an important source of fuel for athletes and while sedentary people will get fat from eating fat, active athletes probably will not. Carbohydrates should remain the foundation of your diet, but should be eaten in balance with protein and fat.

Fruits and vegetables are great sources of complex carbohydrates

Bonking and Hitting the Wall

"Bonking" and "hitting the wall" are terms used by athletes to describe the physical meltdown that occurs when your body runs out of fuel. Bonking occurs when your body's carbohydrate stores are depleted as a result of exercise. As you ride, most of the fuel being burned is used by your muscles, thus taking it away from your other vital organs, which rely on blood glucose. When starting to bonk, your brain and central nervous system become affected and you feel disoriented, tired, irritated, and generally miserable. To remedy the bonk you should eat or drink something that is rich in carbohydrates, or even better yet, avoid the bonk by eating or drinking small amounts periodically while riding.

Hitting the wall is a term used to describe what occurs when the glycogen stores in your muscles have been depleted. As with bonking, you can avoid hitting the wall by consuming fuel periodically while riding, but unlike bonking, once you have hit the wall, you are essentially finished for the day. When this happens, lightheadedness, shaking, disorientation, headaches and loss of body (and, therefore, bike) control set in. This can be a very serious situation. If this happens, get off your bike and start eating and drinking to replenish your fuel stores immediately. This will help reduce the symptoms, but you will only be able to continue very moderate exercise for that day until your muscle glycogen restores itself.

It is wiser to eat smaller amounts of food often, instead of larger amounts less often. Have you ever noticed, after eating a big meal that you are tired and would like to stretch out for a nap? That is the result of your body having to work double-time to metabolize and digest. Consuming less, more frequently, will help keep your glycogen stores at a more consistent level and reduce energy loss during digestion. Some favorite snacks of bikers are bananas, GORP (good old raisins and peanuts), granola mixtures, and pretzels and nuts. You can nibble these easily while spinning down the road.

Hydration

Proper hydration is as important as proper food intake. Your body can lose six pounds (three quarts) of water during an hour of hot-weather exercise. Perspiration is air conditioning for your body — it moves the heat out. And water is the electricity that fuels your body's air conditioner. One rule of thumb to help you avoid dehydration and heat stroke is to drink from your water bottle every fifteen minutes. You should consume about 28 ounces (a standard water bottle) of liquid every hour and more if it is especially hot and humid.

But don't let air temperature fool you. Many people are misled when exercising in cool or wet weather or when on a bike where the wind dries the perspiration, that they are not losing liquid through sweat. Sweat can evaporate quickly under certain conditions, and athletes are as susceptible to dehydration in cooler climes as in hot ones because they are less likely to drink. As mentioned in the previous chapter (page 130), dehydration and heat stroke are serious conditions that can result in hospitalization and even death.

Sports Drinks and Food Supplements

There is a multitude of nutritional supplement products on the market for athletes. These supplements, which come in bars, gels and liquid form, are formulated for quick energy and to restore nutrients lost through extreme physical exertion.

The energy gels have one purpose: to get carbohydrates into your bloodstream the quickest, easiest way possible. Gels are roughly 100 calories of pure carbohydrates. Taken with a big gulp of water, the gel moves quickly from your stomach to your bloodstream, and from there, to your muscles. Energy bars are perfect for calorie and carbohydrate replacement and come in a variety of nutritional combinations, from mainly carbohydrates, to a combination of carbohydrates, protein, and fat. Most are fortified with essential vitamins and minerals, making them perfect snacks when you are on the road. Drink supplements are essential for fluid, potassium and electrolyte replacement and come in powdered or liquid form.

Nutritional supplement and drinks are expensive, so it's a good idea to sample a number of the products before buying mass quantities or multi-gallon refills, as the flavors and consistencies vary and appeal to different tastes.

Preparing Your Meals

Depending on how much cookware and equipment you want to lug along, you have many options for on-the-road meals to replace the calories burned each day. My friend Laurel cooks with fresh foods, never freeze-dried or convenience packed. She purchases home grown fruits and vegetables at farm stands along the way, shops for grains, breads, pasta, cheeses and other vegetarian ingredients at health food stores, and regular groceries at local stores. She usually only buys enough for a meal or two, confident that things will not spoil in her bike bag, and they don't. She makes the entire process look easy, not to mention enjoyable.

Farm stands are wonderful stops along the way

Left to my own devices, I go with the boxed meals that only require the addition of water. Yet there's nothing like a quick stop at a farm stand for a fresh peach or apple — or an occasional restaurant stop. Whatever your plan, be sure to leave some room in your panniers for groceries because you can't always depend on the availability of restaurants.

One of the joys of bike touring is that you can chomp down the calories each day and burn them just as fast. There's no need to count calories — instead, count kilometers or miles.

10/ Camping Along the Way

Some people prefer to stay at motels while on tour, knowing that they can carry less gear on their bikes and sleep in relative luxury. Since this limits your route options, particularly in "tourist areas", most tourers prefer to camp out. My reasons for camping are two: it is much less expensive and it allows me extra outdoor time. My body craves fresh air and the fact that the only walls that surround me while I'm on tour are made of nylon and mosquito netting make returning home to my house a claustrophobic experience. I like the freedom of stopping when and where I choose to end the day.

Private Property

I have a friend who rode his bike across the United States and rarely had to pay for a campsite. An adventuresome sort, Fred would stop in fields, forests, and farms along the way to pitch his tent. If he could find them, he would always ask the owners of the property for permission to set up camp on their land, and rarely was refused. Many times he was invited into homes for the night, to eat with the family, shower and sleep in a comfortable bed. Long-distance bikers are often treated like celebrities, with people happily exchanging food and lodging for some stories of the road. This is a great way to meet the locals and add a new dimension to your touring experience.

I would enjoy communing with local residents on such a level, but it seems more prudent for a woman traveler to set up camp in more commercial settings. Though never fearful of possible dangers, I do try to avoid compromising situations.

Most private landowners are happy to have cyclists camp overnight

State Parks

State parks in the United States usually have designated hiker/biker sites set aside from regular campground traffic for people traveling under their own steam. These tend to be tucked away in a secluded spot far from RVs and cars. The fee for the hike/biker sites ranges from $3.00 to $10.00 a night — nowhere can a better bargain be found. Rarely are hikers or bikers turned away at state parks even if the parks are filled to capacity.

The facilities at state parks are also comfortable. The bathrooms are generally clean and there are hot showers to soak in at the end of the day. Some of these are coin operated, which means you have to have plenty of quarters handy, or you'll end up running back to camp with soapy hair. There are plenty of faucets around the parks with potable water, and an abundance of fire pits and picnic tables. Some parks offer movies and lectures and most have security patrols and a ten o'clock noise curfew, a blessing for early rising bikers.

State and regional parks offer diverse camping sites

The beauty of staying at state parks is the change in scenery. It is always fascinating to me how the landscape of a place can change in fifty-mile distances. Each night that I arrive at a new campsite is like setting foot on a new planet, so diverse is the scenery. Noticing such variety is what makes bike touring so appealing. When traveling in a car, one rarely notices the subtle changes in the land, but on a bike, these differences are rarely missed. Such has always been my experience with the state parks I have visited. Unlike commercial campgrounds, no one looks similar to the ones before it, and each holds its own special beauty.

Where to Find It
Parks and Camping Sites

National Forests & Wilderness Areas
Forest Service
U.S. Department of Agriculture
12th and Independence Street, SW
PO Box 9609
Washington, DC 20090-6090
http://www.fs.fed.us/

National Park Service
1849 C Street, NW
Washington, DC 20240
(202) 208-6843
http://www.nps.gov/parks.html

U. S. State Parks
Search for "state parks"
on any Internet search engine

Campsites in Europe
http://www.interhike.com

Canadian Parks
http://parkscanada.pch.gc.ca/

KOA Sites in U.S, Canada, & Mexico
http://www.koa.com/

Commercial Campgrounds

I have stayed at very few commercial campgrounds during my trips, mainly because the state parks are much more appealing, but I think the best commercial campgrounds I have found in the U.S. are KOAs. I've stayed at them all over the country and have always found their grounds, utilities and shops to be spotlessly clean. They are more expensive than the state park hiker/biker sites, but when forced to use them, you can take advantage of the amenities. There are laundry facilities, hot water dishwashing areas, TV rooms, and sometimes even a hot tub and swimming pools.

Commercial campsites offer many amenities

Sleep

Sleep is nutrition for the body and soul. Some people have a hard time sleeping on the ground, but I find that I am always tired enough to sleep comfortably and soundly through the night. I use a high quality inflatable mattress which protects me from the cold and hardness of the ground. In fact, if you have a down sleeping bag, make sure that you carry an insulated sleeping pad as the feathers beneath you get crushed by your weight, taking away the insulating properties of the bag. For a pillow, you can pack clothes in a stuff sack.

I have camped in some beautiful settings during bike tours. It pays to take a few moments to not only pick a good location, but to make sure, when setting up your tent for the night, that you select a spot that is as free of rocks and roots as possible. Spend some time clearing away sticks and debris — a small stone seems to grow in the night when it's under your mattress. If you are forced to place the tent on protruding objects, make sure the person who is sharing your tent has to sleep on them. Just kidding. Actually, if a completely clear space is unavailable, position yourself so your legs and feet are resting on the debris. Also, if you are forced to erect the tent on an incline, sleep with your head at the higher point.

It's a good idea to leave a flashlight and shoes somewhere nearby in case you have to get up to pee. I always hate getting out of my warm bed/bag to pee in the middle of the night no matter where I am, but stumbling around barefooted in the darkness of your home is a lot safer than in the woods.

It is also a good idea to bring your bags and gear inside of your tent at night. It gets a bit crowded, but the alternative is having animals nose through your bags, or waking up to rain and dew soaked clothing. Make sure your tent is large enough to accommodate both bodies and bags comfortably. . (If you are cycling through bear country, take a page out of the hiker's manual and store your food in a bag suspended from a tree limb — or similar setup.)

Domestic Duties While Camping

OK, you've been riding a bike all day. You're tired, you're hungry, and you're dirty. You want to be fed and bathed and tucked into bed. You want your mommy. But, alas, she's not there. So, fend for yourself you must.

Many a day, upon arriving at camp, I want to stretch out on the picnic table and just pass out until morning. But I know I will wake up hungry, cold and still as smelly as I was when I lay down, so the best way to handle my chores is to do them right away. If you are traveling with a partner, divide up the duties – one can start cooking while the other sets up the tent.

While on tour I make a weekly stop at a laundromat where I fish my dirty clothes out of my bags with a long stick and drop them into the washer with mass quantities of soap. Although I hate doing laundry at home, there is nothing better than having all of those sweaty, smelly, balled-up clothes fresh, sweet smelling and clean. It really brightens your outlook on life. It's a good idea to try to find a laundromat near a grocery store so one person can shop while the other person tends to the washing.

11 / Getting On Your Way

Ok, you've read the book; you've acquired the equipment; you've prepared your bicycle and your body. Now what? Time to tour! I would suggest you start off with a mini-tour before embarking on a trip of greater length so you can get the hang of it. Perhaps you can start with a weekend trip that leaves from and returns to your home, and then you can try a week-long trip.

So, grab a map and trace out a route. Verify the location of campgrounds or motels and make sure they are within a day's riding distance. Pack up your gear! With the exception of clothing, you will have to carry the same amount of gear whether you are on a two-day trip or a two-month trip, but this will be a good opportunity to make sure everything works properly. You might also find, while on a shorter trip, that you need to train more for a longer one—this, too, is good to know before you embark on a longer journey.

Whatever you discover on this shakedown cruise, make sure to have a good time. Enjoy the scenery, enjoy the feeling of the wind on your face, enjoy the sensation of your muscles working, and enjoy the freedom you will feel. Undoubtedly you will be ready to plan a longer journey as soon as you get home.

Glossary of Bicycle Terms

Aerobars - handle bar extensions that allow rider to lean
on forearms, thus gaining a more aerodynamic position.
Allen wrench - solid hexagonal bar, usually L-shaped that fits
into hexagonal hole of an Allen bolt. a.k.a.: hex wrench,
Allen key.
ATB - all terrain bike - another term for mountain bike.
Bar ends - handlebar extensions which mount on ends of
straight handlebars to provide extra hand positions.
Bearings - balls that roll between two parts to make parts
turned. Found in bottom brackets, freewheels, hubs,
headsets and pedals.
Brake levers - hand-held grippers on handlebars used to
apply brakes.
Brake pads - rubber pads that connect with tire rim to slow
bike down.
Braze-ons - small fittings permanently attached to frame
such as cable guides, water bottle cage mounts, pump
attachments.
Bottle cage - metal or plastic holder for water bottle that is
attached to frame.
Bottom bracket - part of frame around which pedal cranks
revolve and the bearings and axle assembly which runs
through it.
Cables - wires used to control gears and brakes.
Cable housing - plastic tube through which cables run.
Cantilever brakes - brakes with two separate arms, one on
each side of rim. Each pivots independently of the other.

Cassette – refers to cluster of sprockets that make up freewheel.

Center-pull brakes – brakes in which cable runs down center line of bike, using a yoke to connect to center point of brake.

Century – a 100 mile ride.

Chain ring – front sprocket on bike.

Chainstay – tapered tube running from bottom bracket to rear fork ends.

Chain remover – a tool used to remove and replace pins holding chain links together.

Clipless pedals – pedals similar to ski bindings in which cleat on shoes locks into pedal mechanism and is released by twist of foot.

Cogs – sprockets on rear of bike.

Crankset – the components which make up a crankset are two pedal cranks and chainwheels.

Crescent wrench – angle-headed wrench, in adjustable or fixed styles.

Derailleur – gear changing mechanism.

Downtube – frame tube running diagonally from bottom bracket to lower end of head tube.

Drop handlebars – handlebars found on road and touring bikes that drop down in 's' position. a.k.a. *road handlebars.*

Dual suspension bike – (dualie) mountain bike with suspension in front and back.

Fork – part of frame that holds wheel.

Freewheel – mechanism that makes coasting possible. Comes with rear cogs or sprockets attached.

Granny gears – term referring to lowest gears on bike, used for climbing hills.

Grip shifters – shifting mechanism on mountain or hybrid bikes in which rider grips and turns a portion of the handlebar to change gears.

Handlebar stem - part that connects the handlebar to the steering mechanism of the fork.

Hardtail - a mountain bike with no suspension in rear.

Headset - bearing assembly that connect front fork to frame and allows handlebar to turn.

Hybrid - a mountain bike/touring bike combination, usually with upright handlebar positioning.

Hubs - middle part of wheel - the axle and shell.

Knobbies - thick tires with knobs or bumps used to gain better traction. Found on mountain bikes.

Pannier - Bag attached to wheel area used for touring.

Presta valve - narrow valve on tire tube that has a built-in, screw down top. Used with high performance bike tubes. Requires an adapter in order to fit regular pump heads.

Quick release - component that allows for removal of wheels without use of wrenches or other tools.

Rapid-fire shifters - also known as thumb shifters. Located on mountain bike handlebars in a position where hands don't have to move to shift.

Recumbent bicycle - a bike that allows rider to sit in a chair with feet pedaling out in front. Steering done with feet and rider sits low to ground.

Rim - portion of wheel that holds tire and allows for braking.

Road bars - a.k.a. drop handlebars.

Road bike - refers to lighter weighted bikes ridden on road, usually for racing, having drop handlebars.

SAG Wagon - (Support and Gear.) Vehicle used to carry gear for touring riders and transport riders who need a lift.

Seat post - tube that holds seat in frame.

Shrader valve - older fashioned, wider stemmed valve on tire tubes, usually found on utility or kids' bikes.

Side-pull brakes - brakes which function with a cable running down to one side of the component.

Soft tail – mountain bike with rear suspension.

Spoke – thin strands of metal used to lace wheel rims.

Spoke wrench – a tool used to adjust/remove wheel spokes.

Sprocket – toothed wheel part of chain drive.

Third hand – a clamping tool used to hold brake shoes tight against rim to make brake cable adjustment easier.

Tire irons – small levers used to pry tire away from rim to allow removal of tube.

Tire valve – stem to which pump attached to allow tube to be filled with air.

Toe clips – metal or plastic cages attached to pedals in which foot is inserted and held firmly with an adjustable strap.

Top tube – portion of frame that runs horizontally from seat to headset.

Wedge pack – small pack that attaches behind seat.

Wheel dropout – open end on forks that allow for easy release of wheels.

Index

Other Books from Vitesse Press

Cycling Along The Canals of New York by Louis Rossi $15.95
500 miles of cycling along the Erie, Champlain, and Cayuga-Seneca canals.

Bicycle Road Racing by Edward Borysewicz $24.95
A complete road-racing program by former National Coach Eddie B.

Massage For Cyclists by Roger Pozeznik $14.95
Clear advice and excellent photos of massage sequences. 2nd Printing.

Mountain Biking For Women by Robin Stuart & Cathy Jensen $15.00
Woman to woman advice and instruction from two experienced cyclists.

Central New York Mountain Biking by Dick Mansfield $12.95
Thirty of the best back road and trail rides in upstate New York.

Vermont Mountain Biking by Dick Mansfield $10.95
Twenty-four rides in southern Vermont.

Fit and Pregnant by Joan Butler $16.00
Advice from a nurse-midwife who is an athlete and mother. Fifth printing.

Cycling Health and Physiology by Ed Burke, PH.D. $17.95
Using sports science to improve your riding and racing (2nd edition)

Canoe Racing by Peter Heed $14.95
The "bible" of flat water canoe racing. Third printing.

We encourage you to buy our books at a bookstore or sports shop. When ordering directly from Vitesse, prepayment or a credit card number and expiration date is required. Please include the price of the book plus handling ($2.50 for the first book, $1.00 for each additional book) and 5% sales tax for Vermont addresses.

Telephone   802-229-4243   Fax   802-229-6939
Postal Orders:
VITESSE PRESS, PMB 367, 45 State Street, Montpelier, VT 05601-2100

Email: dick@vitessepress.com   Web site: www.vitessepress.com